HIDDEN TREASURES

WALES

Edited by Lynsey Hawkins

First published in Great Britain in 2002 by
YOUNG WRITERS
Remus House,
Coltsfoot Drive,
Peterborough, PE2 9JX
Telephone (01733) 890066

HB ISBN 0 75434 108 9
SB ISBN 0 75434 109 7

FOREWORD

This year, the Young Writers' Hidden Treasures competition proudly presents a showcase of the best poetic talent from over 72,000 up-and-coming writers nationwide.

Young Writers was established in 1991 and we are still successful, even in today's technologically-led world, in promoting and encouraging the reading and writing of poetry.

The thought, effort, imagination and hard work put into each poem impressed us all, and once again, the task of selecting poems was a difficult one, but nevertheless, an enjoyable experience.

We hope you are as pleased as we are with the final selection and that you and your family continue to be entertained with *Hidden Treasures Wales* for many years to come.

CONTENTS

Sam Stafford	34
Jake Evans	34
David Roberts	35
Joshua Gethin	35
Thomas Herbert	36
Madeleine Hughes	36
Alex Newnes	37
Hannah Cullen-Jones	37
Shaun Williams	38
Emma Edwards	38
Sophie Howells	39
Jonathan Roberts	39
Matthew Jack Newnes	40
Alisha Gethin	40
Bethany Roberts	41
Holly Bevan	41
Sam Hewitt	42
Robert Anderson	42
Sabrina Pinchera	42
Benjamin Keith Roberts	43
Owen Lloyd	43

Gelli Primary School, Pentre

Connie Price	44
Lauren Davies	45
Calum Thomas	46
Shaun Davies	46
Matthew Noster	46
Jodie Matthews	47
Phoebe Owen	47
Amy Jones	47
Matthew Griffiths	48
Jamie Fear	49
Tristan Foley	50
Emily Farr	51
Georgia Macey	51
Katie Hannah Bevan	52
Rebecca Wigley	52

Griag y Wion Primary School, Pontypridd

Guilsfield CP School, Welshpool

Bertie Jones	66
Hannah Russell	67
Jackson Lee-Jones	67
Helen Morgan	68
Lyndsey Jones	68
Lynzee-Kim Sinden	69
Jessica Thomas	69
Bethany Wilcox	70
Lucy Gwilt	71
Jade Griffiths	72
Katie Davies	72
Beverley Lloyd	73
Katie Gittins	73
James Hatton	74
Philip White	74
Matthew Jones	75
Richelle Griffin	76
Emma Graham	76
Emma Davies	77
Lowri Evans	78
Philip Hughes	78
Laura Mary Sinclair	79
Madeleine Carver	80
Laura Speake	81
Abbie Gittins	82
Jennifer Morgan	82
Joel William Dyos	83
Sophie Bough	83
Jenny Lewis	84
Rhiannon Jones	85
Jennie Morris	86
Lucy Davies	87

Hirwaun Primary School, Aberdare

James Morgan	87
Benjamin Duckham	88
Samantha Maria Elias	88

Rhys Jones	89
Stacey Louise Kerr	89
Alicia Ewington	90
Corey Addiscott	90
Stephanie Abraham	91
Lorren Daily	91
Samantha Brookman	92
Benjamin Barnett	92
James Shilton	93
Lauren Lewis	93
Ashlee Evans	94
Martyn Thomas Bell	94
Dominic Silva	95
Sara Busby	95
Rebecca Jayne Wilkins	96
Laura Davies	96
Selina May David	97
Emily Jones	97
Michaela Pedro	97
John Mullaney	98
James Smith	98
Ellisha Nadine Hughes	98
Fenn Moss-Izzard	99
Natasha Eynon	99

Libanus CP School, Brecon

Rachel Perry	100
Harry Lowles	100
Jenny Jones	101
Mariah Chapman	101
Luke Jackson	102
Emma Samuel	102
Katie Jones	103
Jessica Holroyd	104

Llanfaes Community Primary School, Brecon

Ben Miles	105
Alexander Griffiths	106

The Poems

MY SCHOOL

Pack your bag, don't be late,
Make sure you've got your homework;
Arrive at school, sit at your desk,
Answer your name at the register,
Get out your pens to do your maths,
2x3, 5x8, oh I'm so confused
And now it's nearly play time;
Come in from play,
It's time to do gym,
Forward rolls and stretches galore,
I wish we had time to do more,
Let's go in for food,
Followed by play,
That's the end of the day.

Leigh Southall (11)
Aberdare Town CW Primary School, Aberdare

THE PIRATE SHIP

More battle awaiting,
The sun all arose,
'The cannons need dusting'
The captain supposed,
The ship with a wound,
The water gushed in
'A perfect day for winning'
Said the pole man with glee.
But how wrong was the crew,
As the ship started to sink
And the crew took a chance
And swam to the bank,
But the war wasn't done.

David Griffiths (11)
Aberdare Town CW Primary School, Aberdare

DRAGON BIRTH

In the mists of long ago,
On the tallest mountain,
There stood a pine tree forest.
In the pine tree forest,
There grew an old pine tree.
Under the pine tree,
There lay a pile of fallen needles.
Beneath these needles,
Was a magic hole,
Inside this magic hole,
Lay a round grey stone.
Underneath this round grey stone,
There lay a colourful egg
And in this egg,
There was a deep crack.
From that crack flew a hot breath,
From that breath,
There came a sudden breeze of fire.
From that bright fire . . .

A baby dragon was born!

Cora Green (10)
Aberdare Town CW Primary School, Aberdare

FAMILIES

Just an ordinary day,
With more to be gained,
Old people, young babies, animals and birds,
Smiling and waving, people greeting the world.

Hip hop and pop,
Modern music and jazz,
Until the day ends,
There's new experiences to be had.

An ordinary day, there's no such thing,
Daytime is ending, darkness fills the sky.
All the chores are taken care of,
One more day passes by.

Vans and cars are parked up for the night,
Inside the houses, people are curled up tight,
Endless dreams, peaceful and sweet.

Joshua Jarvis (11)
Aberdare Town CW Primary School, Aberdare

ON A SATURDAY

My friend sleeps up on a Friday night,
We watch horror movies, it fills us with fright.
We wake up early to watch videos,
Then my friend has to go home.
But this week is different as my father's away,
I normally go to his house on this faithful day,
My Saturdays are really quite fun,
As I get a trip away from my mum.
Because I am home, I don't get a trip,
So I put on my coat and pull up my zip.
I go down the library to borrow some books,
I read about inventors, plumbers and cooks.
I come home early, around one o'clock,
I put on my slippers and take off my socks.
Then I go in the lounge to watch TV,
I switch right over to the BBC,
I get into my bed and fall asleep,
My mother comes in and I don't make a peep.

Mitchell Tennant (11)
Aberdare Town CW Primary School, Aberdare

THE WORLD AS WE SEE IT

Some time was old,
Older than gold,
The world was created,
The food was baited,
To lure the creatures in,
Surely we have been
Here for years and years.
The revelations fares,
Have cost the world its cares,
Now even through its tears,
Could have been repairs,
We'll do our best
To save the rest,
But many thinkers sit on chairs,
Not doing very much,
Caring some for recycling,
Not much for biking,
But the favours who do,
You can help too!

Charlotte Lippard (11)
Aberdare Town CW Primary School, Aberdare

CHRISTMAS

The snow falls thick and fast,
As Christmas has arrived at last.
Tonight the man all dressed in red,
Will visit us while we are in bed.
Under the tree the pressies lay,
Waiting for us on Christmas Day.

Thomas Anderson (10)
Aberdare Town CW Primary School, Aberdare

SPRING, SUMMER AND WINTER

Spring, summer and winter too,
We always have to go to school,
No matter what the weather, no matter how you feel.

But the one thing that we guarantee is you'll always see a smile,
Because smiling is contagious,
You'll catch one like the flu
When someone smiled at me in school,
I had to smile back too.

But when the day is over
And I'm glad to be going home.
I walk around the corner and Mrs Gardner sees me grin
And when she smiled,
I realised I'd passed a smile on again.

Amy Evans (11)
Aberdare Town CW Primary School, Aberdare

CHRISTMAS

Christmas is a happy time,
With lots of things to do,
Buying gifts for friends we know,
With cards to send off too.
In every house lights twinkle,
It's nice to see the glow,
With Christmas trees and holly,
My thoughts turn to snow.
I wish it would snow for Christmas,
How happy I would be,
I could make a snowman,
To join my family.

Chelsea Lawrence (11)
Aberdare Town CW Primary School, Aberdare

EVERY NIGHT

Every night when the moon is full
And the hairs stand up on the top of your skull.
The appalling beast with the hideous face,
Invites all brutish types to his place.

The witches with their witchy tricks,
Come flying in on witchy sticks.
They swerve to the left and they swerve to the right,
Flying dangerously all through the night.

The goblins come on the dragons back
And the werewolves, hmph! They just follow the track.
The ghouls and ghosts in ghastly guises,
Race as the zombie slowly rises.

By now the party's in full swing,
The skeletons start to do their thing.
Bones go flying here and there,
Now they can't dance cos they have no bones to spare.

It's midnight now, but nobody is tired,
Though the kitchen has gone crazy and a frog has been fired.
With the beast's face melting and some bats brains on the floor,
Everybody's screaming and heading for the door.

So now the beast is liquid
And the goblins are having their ride,
Let's forget about this party
And the next'll be outside.

Christopher Millard (11)
Aberdare Town CW Primary School, Aberdare

WALES

Wales is where I come from
Known as the land of song
Where Tom Jones, Shirley Bassey, The Stereophonics and
Charlotte Church also come.

Our emblem is the yellow daffodil,
Which is often seen flowering on the hill.
Sometimes covering the old mine seam,
Where miners mined the coal,
The only job for men and their sons,
Many years ago.

Once we were also famous for our rugby,
But now the Millennium Stadium outshines our national team,
This fantastic building has put the Welsh Dragon back on the map,
Where Castle Coach stands out high above the A470,
A landmark before we enter Cardiff.

Wales is where I come from,
I'm very proud of that,
Our heritage and friendship,
Will always shine through, that's a fact,
Though many changes will occur,
Now the National Assembly is in tact,
No matter where I travel or roam,
There will always be a hiraeth for Wales
The green, green grass of home.

Owain Gwillim (11)
Aberdare Town CW Primary School, Aberdare

THE STAR THAT SHONE

In the pitch-black sky there were many stars,
But there was one in particular that caught my eye.

It shone like a brand new diamond,
Which had been just discovered by a poor, old miner.

It shone like a street like all alone in a city,
Which lit up the streets at night.

It shone like a candle in an old man's house,
All that comforted him was that bright light.

The next morning my star had disappeared,
I hope tonight it will be there again shining as it did but
Brighter than it shone last night.

Anna Brockway (11)
Aberdare Town CW Primary School, Aberdare

CYMRU AM BYTH

C   ardiff is Wales' capital city,
Y   es its castle is very pretty,
M   ind you, all of Wales is beautiful too,
R   eally green valleys, which rivers run through,
U   p mountains like Snowdon, the air is so sweet

A   nd down the mines, there's still gold underfeet.
M   y favourite place though, in all of this land,

B   ecause of my love of the sea and the sand,
Y   ou know, it's the Gower, along Swansea Bay,
T   he seagulls and boats, I could watch them all day.
H   ome's where the heart is, and mine is in Wales.

Robyn Davies (11)
Aberdare Town CW Primary School, Aberdare

HIDDEN TREASURE

Up in the attic, covered in dust,
I found an old iron trunk full of rust,
I wondered what was in this rusty old case,
So I took it to a secret place.

I took it to a really old house,
Where I saw a very, very big mouse,
When I saw its long furry tail,
I scared myself and I went pale.

I played and fiddled with the lock,
Then I gave it a good hard knock,
When it opened I had a surprise,
Right before my very eyes,
There was a little wooden toy,
That my grandad had lost when he was a boy.

Craig Mallett (11)
Aberdare Town CW Primary School, Aberdare

A BEAUTIFUL DAY

The sky so blue, the sun so bright,
A boy runs past flying a kite.
Flowers so pretty, so many to see,
Yellow, blue, pink and green.

The birds tweet so very sweet,
The grass is smooth, like green sheets,
I spy a ladybird with all her spots,
She has with her some babies, lots and lots.

Today has been a beautiful day,
I hope tomorrow is the same I pray.

Charlotte Scorey (11)
Aberdare Town CW Primary School, Aberdare

FOOTBALL

Ten o'clock on Saturday,
It's football time again.
I warm up with the others
To be in the seven out of ten.

I wait for the decision,
The coach's face has a frown.
I feel quite nervous waiting
As he looks us up and down.

He points his finger quickly
At each child he has chosen,
We're all shaking in our boots now,
But not because we're frozen.

My name's called out eventually,
I feel shaky and excited.
The football shirts are given out,
At last we are united.

United as a team we stand,
Listening to the team talk.
I'm to stay right back in defence,
Remembering to run not walk.

The game at last is over,
But filthy and shattered,
We drink our drinks and wipe our sweat,
We had the win that mattered.

Geraint Crawley (11)
Aberdare Town CW Primary School, Aberdare

MY DOG GUNNER

This is a dog who has four white paws,
He has a wrinkle on his nose.
This a dog who gets dirty paws,
When he does, out he goes.

Trouble that's no surprise,
With those big, sad eyes,
With his big chubby cheeks
And his attention he always seeks.

He chews his hedgehog,
That squeaks all day long,
He nibbles the cheese out of his kong.
He likes to play, he likes to fight,
His bark will give you such a fright.

He barks at the cats
And chases the rats,
Everyone talks
About how he takes us for walks.

With his ferocious teeth,
He causes mischief,
But he means no harm,
He is sometimes calm.

As someone walks through the door,
He always gets excited,
So come and see my dog Gunner,
You're all invited.

Alex Biggs (11)
Aberdare Town CW Primary School, Aberdare

A DAY AT THE SEASIDE

We packed our bus with food and toys,
For all us little girls and boys,
With suncream on our arms and legs
And little straw hats on our heads,
The teachers said, 'All stay together,
We must take care in this hot weather.'

We found the sea and golden sand,
With melting ice cream in our hands,
Buckets, spades, bats and ball,
A brilliant time was had by all,
The fairground noises cast their spells,
With bumper cars and carousels.

With pockets full of sand and shells,
I hear the sounds of our school bells,
My teacher's waiting at the gate,
It was all a dream, but it was great.

Corie Sewell (11)
Aberdare Town CW Primary School, Aberdare

WHAT?

What will this world be with no care?
What would this world be with no air?
What will be left to keep us healthy?
When I'm grown up
What will this world become?

What will these reptiles see in this world?
Now in 2002 we are lucky,
What will this world be?

Ashley James Vardon (11)
Aberdare Town CW Primary School, Aberdare

PIRATE

The sun is shining really bright,
Only sand and sea in sight.
A cross mark to spot on the map,
I wish the chest was on my lap,
Rubies, diamonds, silver, gold,
Treasure's I wish to have and hold.
A hook and parrot are with me,
Sailing upon the big blue sea,
Follow the map across the sand,
My treasure is close at my hand,
Dig and dig, hope to see all the
Treasure, will be for me.

Donna Day (11)
Aberdare Town CW Primary School, Aberdare

YOU AND ME

You see dull skies, horrible, dark skies,
I see bright skies and my favourite colour blue,
You hear flies, bees and wasps,
Landing and flying around your head,
I hear the sound of trains,
Puffing on the tracks,
You walk like a baby,
I walk happy and cool,
You sing sad, leaving songs,
I sing joyful, happy songs,
You feel like you are leaving,
I feel like I am starting afresh,
I wish you could be like me.

Gareth Nickels (8)
Abertaf Primary School, Abercynon

WHEN AUTUMN COMES

When autumn comes
Hear buzzards squawking
When autumn comes
Feel mud on my feet
When autumn comes
See owls swooping for their prey
When autumn comes
Smell smoke from fireworks
When autumn comes
Dark nights close in
And winter creeps behind.

Ben Instrell (8)
Abertaf Primary School, Abercynon

YOU AND ME

You see strangers, frowns and blackness,
I see friends, sunsets and kindness,
You hear screams, storms and slapping,
I hear laughter, football and pencil's drawing,
You sing lullabies, funeral marches and the blues,
I sing pop music, old music and dancing music,
You walk slouched over trembling and shaking,
I walk groovy, cool and with a swing,
You feel unhappy, alone and scared,
I feel good, excited and jumpy,
I wish I could give these things to you.

Jack Perkins (9)
Abertaf Primary School, Abercynon

YOU AND ME

I see the sun shining,
You see the rain falling down,
I hear the noises from chattering people,
You hear the silence,
Because you are lonely,
I sing loud and funny,
You sing sadly with a choir,
I feel a warm breeze,
You feel a sharp wind,
I feel happy and joyful,
You feel sad and lonely,
I skip, dance and play,
You walk dragging your tail,
I dance to pop music,
You dance to nothing,
I sleep in a warm bed,
You sleep on the street,
I wish you could be like me.

Chelsey Breakingbury (9)
Abertaf Primary School, Abercynon

AN AUTUMN FEAST

Sprinkle some brown crispy leaves
Add the orange of a morning sky
Chop up a golden moon
Beat in the flames of a roaring bonfire
Pour in some nice cool rain
Gather three glittering stars
Orange of the evening sky
Red of the woodland toadstools
Bake altogether for an autumn feast.

Katie Smart (8)
Abertaf Primary School, Abercynon

CHANGES

Would you like to have walked
Through the streets of Abercynon past?
Saw miners huffing and puffing,
Swinging and sweating,
Digging down in the deep, dark, dirty mines.
Seen steam engines swooping and rolling
Through the green and rainbowed valleys.
Listened to the 'Clock' school bells,
Saying 'Time to start the day.'

Life is so much faster now,
Cars run like cheetahs through town.
No sleepy Sundays,
Just shoppers rushing by,
Adults running with chattering children,
To busy clubs and schools.

I wonder when I walk
Through the streets of Abercynon's future
If I will see floating cars
Millions more people getting better jobs?
Or maybe we'll have a thrilling and fascinating museum
Showing Abercynon's exciting past.

Stacey Jones (9)
Abertaf Primary School, Abercynon

RED

Red is the colour of my pet goldfish, when it's swimming around,
Red is the colour of a heart when you're in love,
Red is the colour of a telephone box, where I make my secret calls,
Red is the colour of paint as it drips off the wall.

Red is the colour of my mother's lips, when she is going out,
Red is the colour of ripe, shiny apples as they hang from the tree,
Red is the colour of Christmas lights, that decorate the windows,
Red is the colour of a robin's breast, as he flies in the cold, cold breeze,
Red is the colour that makes me feel hot.

Kristi Murphy (9)
Abertaf Primary School, Abercynon

RED

Red is the colour of my beating heart and my speaking lips,
Red is the colour of temper, madness and fury,
Red is the colour of a Rhagfyr sunset as I close my curtains,
Red is the colour of a robin's breast,
Red is the colour of an autumn tree with crispy leaves, ready to fall,
Red is the colour of a winning Welsh flag,
A sea of people cheering,
Red is the colour of a blushing face when a boy asks you to dance.

Rachel Murphy (8)
Abertaf Primary School, Abercynon

RED

Red is my favourite colour,
It is warm and makes me feel happy and joyful,
Red is the colour of my loving heart
And my shiny lips.
Red is the colour of fire,
Red is the colour of my pencil case,
Where I keep my riches.

Natalie Jenkins (9)
Abertaf Primary School, Abercynon

SHADOW

S neaking behind you,
H ow does it get there?
A big black creature walking behind
D oes it go away?
O h! It's really spooky,
W atch out!

Rebecca Robinson (8)
Abertaf Primary School, Abercynon

THE SUN

Roasting sun, hot and bright,
Shining down on us,
Blinding, shimmering sun,
Sparkling as bright as it can.
Beaming down rays of light.

Christopher Stonelake (8)
Blaengwawr Primary School, Aberdare

ROMAN SOLDIER

Roman soldier marching to battle,
A courageous soldier,
Enemies dying for help.
Straight and wiry,
Taking countries over,
War killing soldiers,
Scary Cells,
Coming nearer,
Attacking them,
Killing them.

Carys Evans (8)
Blaengwawr Primary School, Aberdare

ROMAN SOLDIER

Amazing, hard soldier
Brave and strong,
Hard shining shield,
Reflecting the bright sun.
Healthy, muscular soldier,
Attacking the scary enemy,
Wild and angry.

Justine Sysum (8)
Blaengwawr Primary School, Aberdare

THE SEA EXPLORER

When I go into the clear blue sea,
I swim right and left,
I go in a shiny submarine,
With sharks gathering around me and swimming away,
I see blood all around,
An abandoned ship,
Dead bodies in it,
I go to the surface with lots of news.

Elliot Baker (8)
Blaengwawr Primary School, Aberdare

ROMAN SOLDIER

Shield shining in the sun,
Strong and amazing soldier.
Wild enemy, fighting him to the death,
Angry soldier, muscular,
Brave and amazing soldier,
Sad and tired.

Megan Thomas (8)
Blaengwawr Primary School, Aberdare

ROMAN SOLDIERS

Shields shining in the sun,
Spears flying through the air,
Romans marching into battle,
Stabbing enemies,
Killing soldiers,
Bearing heavy metal,
Sharp swords,
Big muscles,
Good strong arms,
Fully trained,
Mighty and fearless.

Jordan George (8)
Blaengwawr Primary School, Aberdare

ROMAN SOLDIERS

Strong Roman soldiers,
Marching through the village,
Brave and powerful.
Fighting enemies in battles,
Courageous soldiers
Stabbing with their sharp spears
Against their frightening enemy.
Shields protecting Roman soldiers,
Fighting the army with daggers,
Heroic and brave,
Plucky and strong.

Craig Williams (8)
Blaengwawr Primary School, Aberdare

THE ANGRY WHALE

I am part of sea life,
Not a monster,
I swim sadly in the sea
As my mum has been captured,
I can't bear to think of my mum
Being torn to pieces just for her fat.

I feel afraid and helpless because I
Know that one day that will be me.

I can smell oil in the sea,
All of the fish are dead,
There are hundreds of seals
On shore covered in oil.

I can hear dolphins and whales
Crying for help.

Nearly all of the whales are extinct,
We are dying because humans are capturing us,
My sister is in shows in a small pool,
She hates it because the pool is so small that she can't
Move and the humans laugh at her,
She wants to be free and live happily in the sea.
Most of my brothers and sisters have been
Captured or put in shows.

I'm just asking for one simple thing - to be free.

Emma Wilding (10)
Coed-y-Lan Primary School, Pontypridd

THE TIGER'S THOUGHTS

People look at me and run,
My huge white teeth and claws judge me straight away,
But no! They judge me wrong, I am a graceful, beautiful creature.

It's my coat and teeth that are the problem,
Men hunt me with guns and traps.

As I glide through the jungle, running for my life,
I hear gunshots echoing around me,
The footsteps of the men thudding on the floor,
I'm terrified my life is on the line.

There's nowhere to go, nowhere to hide,
Men everywhere,
It's as if I'm trapped in my own home,
My family and me are in real danger of extinction.

I don't like killing but I have to, for survival,
I just wish you could hear me call,
To make you realise how we tigers feel.

Jacob Fosterjohn (11)
Coed-y-Lan Primary School, Pontypridd

THE ELEPHANT'S ADVICE

I'm scared of you
But I know I could kill you
With my extremely powerful tusks
You will kill us for them
But what have I ever done to you?

Let me be free in the wastelands of Africa and India
But my cousins are worse off in the circus
And in the zoo, lazing around in a cramped cage
We haven't put you in a cage
Or made you do tricks in front of my herd.

I've never taken your teeth or bones
And so why do you do it to us?
I am just a grey object to you
Roaming in fear.

Rhys Evans (10)
Coed-y-Lan Primary School, Pontypridd

DREADFUL GRAVEYARD

In the graveyard, misty with dread
Nightmares come to your head.

Ghosts jump out and make you shout,
They are always lurking about!

In the graveyard, misty with dread,
Nightmares come to your head.

They dive into houses, through the walls,
Scare children with their caterwauls.

In the graveyard, misty with dread,
Nightmares come to your head.

Rotted away each body they call home,
In the day they vanish but at dusk, they roam.

In the graveyard, misty with dread,
Nightmares come to your head.

In the day they vanish away till
Dusk when they roam . . . to torment us!

Ross Games (11)
Cwmdu School, Cwmdu

WIND OF COLOURS

Wind of colours, wind of light,
Glistening in the moon twilight.
If you look into the sky you will see the wind
Way up high
Brightening everything that's dark and after
That it'll leave a mark.
Mark of yellow, mark of blue,
Mark of orange and red too.
The brightness of silver, the shine of gold,
The night now is getting old,
The night starts to shrink away and the
Sun comes up for the break of day.
The wind of colours fade, it's gone,
There was a wind of colours
But now there's none.

Haydn Williams (10)
Cwmdu School, Cwmdu

A WINTER WALK

I tread my way through the wood,
Golden red leaves make a carpet fit for a king.
I glance up through the leafless trees,
The blue sky blinks down at me.
The cold glittering river runs by my feet,
I see a squirrel scampering in the trees.
It's growing darker and the red sunset
Grabs me into its magic world.
The mountains are tall, the sun's sinking lower,
Night has come and I make my way home.
I hear an owl toot high above me,
I see a rabbit run through the bare trees.

Laura Watkins (11)
Cwmdu School, Cwmdu

PEGASUS

Pegasus was raised by no mortal mare
But by Neptune the sea god in his despair.
Dark droplets of blood from Medusa's snaky severed head
Combined with salt sea foam - thus Pegasus was bred.
This powerful winged steed was so dazzling bright
Upon him the sun god chased away night.
Gifted with immortal life and incredible speed
He would help Bellerophon in his hour of need
To hunt the monster, Chimaera, a terrible beast
Devouring each night a human for its foul feast.
To tame Pegasus to mortal rider required great skill
And Minerva's golden bridle to bend the horse to his will.
They galloped through the air, seeing kingdoms below
Ravaged and ransacked, filled only with woe,
The monster was prowling with dragon tail beating,
Lion mouth breathing fire, prepared for this meeting.
Bellerophon swung at the goat - body with his sword
But the great beast twisted and at Pegasus clawed
Hoping the soft white skin to slash and tear
But the brave-hearted Pegasus did not scare,
Striking with great hooves he reared in attack.
The monster struggled to drive him back.
Bellerophon hacked with his sword for hours
Its blood flowing freely Chimaera losing its powers
Sinks to the sand with its life ebbing away -
Just as the dark night is defeated by day.

Emily Ham (11)
Cwmdu School, Cwmdu

CARTOONS: WHAT A LOT OF NONSENSE!

Mickey Mouse has big ears,
He has been around for years,
Disney's Mr Smee has a big belly
And a sewer is very smelly,
Captain Hook is a crook
Water flows down a brook,
Daffy Duck is barking mad
Pluto is so very sad.
Dennis the Menace hates tennis,
My nan's gardener is called Glenys,
Goofy has big, big feet,
They are longer than the longest street!
Captain Pugwash is a fool,
He sank his ship in a paddling pool.
The Clangers are all head bangers,
They eat garage, loads of spanners,
Tom and Jerry wreck the house,
All because Tom wants a mouse!

Joseph Parry (11)
Cwmdu School, Cwmdu

BROTHERS

Brothers . . . Who wants them? Brothers are pains
If you are the youngest brother you always get blamed
When you did nothing . . . you haven't done right
Brothers nag at you when you change the TV channel
Brothers always start a fight!
Brothers always get better stuff than you do
Brothers never play your games
Brothers are pains!

Adam Farrell (11)
Cwmdu School, Cwmdu

NIGHT FRIGHT!

Early in the morning, before the world's awake,
The old tree looks like a cold stick man by my gate,
Mr Frost's icy fingers at my window try to slide in,
The darkness is scaring me.
What is out there?
Suddenly a ray of light shines in my eyes,
It is the sun that wakes the world,
The world is warming and stirring to life,
Frost's fingers lose their grip,
Slipping into water for the flowers.
Light and heat destroy the cruelness of the dark
And colours come bursting with the powers of the light
I hear the first sound of the cockerel crowing
The morning has killed my night fright!

Daniel Inglefield (10)
Cwmdu School, Cwmdu

INVENTIONS

Wouldn't it be great to invent something new!
A singing wristwatch, an automatic broom.
The things you could invent, the list goes on and on . . .
A non-melting chocolate, an everlasting bonbon.
If I invented stuff like this I would be rich,
But then every single invention would have a hitch.
The automatic broom would not know when to stop,
The singing wristwatch would break with one raindrop,
The non-melting chocolate would crack teeth with great ease,
The everlasting bonbon, I don't think will please,
So none of my inventions have got a good swing,
It looks like I'll have to go back to dreaming!

Andrew Nicholls (10)
Cwmdu School, Cwmdu

THE GOAT

The goat's coat is as brown as chocolate,
With spots on his back, white as the snows,
His eyes are blue, as blue as the ocean,
With his stumpy horns, he chases the crows.

He munches his hay and his feed full of oats,
His hooves are black, as black as coal,
He thumps the ground when he's in a mood,
He gets very muddy when he starts to roll.

The goat's coat is as brown as chocolate,
Now no spots on his back as white as snow,
The fox is creeping as slow as you grow,
The goat has been bitten - red blood starts to flow.

Kirstie Grattidge (10)
Cwmdu School, Cwmdu

GO-CART

I really want to own a go-cart,
The only wish in my deepest heart,
I'd like it to have a powerful engine
So I can drive around with a great big grin
Chanting peace and serenity
(I've always wanted to be a hippy)
But that is getting away from the point
I'll need some oil for the artic' joint
My telephone number's 611 822
But just send a letter if I'm close to you
I am prepared to come and collect
But it can't be far,
'Cause I haven't got a go-cart yet.

Thomas Foster (10)
Cwmdu School, Cwmdu

AVALANCHE!

Like an
Explosion
The avalanche starts.
It
Comes crashing
Down the hill
Crushing
What is in its way?
The only noise
You hear is
The sound of it
Smashing trees
And a *bang*
Bang, bang, bang!
As it throws rocks
Down the valley.

Howell Williams (8)
Cwmdu School, Cwmdu

THE HUNTER'S POEM

Sprawling, crawling through the grass,
Ready for the wolves that pass,
Aiming with his evil gun
After this the wolf won't run!
Just about to pull the trigger
With his evil cunning snigger.
The cold bullet hits
On the wolf, there's a bleeding slit,
The hunter has an evil soul,
In his heart there is a hole.

Oliver Bowler (10)
Cwmdu School, Cwmdu

THE SHARK

The silent hunter of the deep
Whenever you're nearby, they always take a peep,
In the sea they are all mighty,
The hammerheads are all fighty,
Attack you they may not,
But in the sea there are a lot!
Sharks, the silent hunters of the deep,
Next time you're swimming in the sea,
Don't go too deep!

Craig Parry (10)
Cwmdu School, Cwmdu

SOUNDS

I hate the sound of an avalanche,
When it crashes and dashes against the rocks,
I hate the sound of a bee buzz, buzzing
Inside the house,
I hate the sound of a tree falling down
And the sound of it hitting the ground.
I like the sound of an owl going tu-whit tu-whoo,
I like the sound of a ghost calling 'Ooo,ooo!'
I like the sound of a snake ssss!
I like the sound of a clock's ticking tick-tock.

Joe Robins (8)
Cwmdu School, Cwmdu

MY PETS

My dog's fur is as soft as wool,
My dog's tongue is as rough as a pine cone,
My dog's bark is loud as a storm wind blowing a door,
My dog's tail wags like a flag.

My cat's purr is like scissors cutting paper,
My cat's eyes are green as leaves moving on a tree,
My cat's miaow sounds like the wind howling,
My cat's whiskers are like wire.

Lydia Williams (8)
Cwmdu School, Cwmdu

OUR FARM

The hay in the barn rustles
When the wind whistles,
Our dogs snore when they sleep
On scrumpled straw in a heap.
The bull snorts, squelching, squishy mud
While the farmer's bobcat moves manure
And it splashes from side to side in the bucket.
Trees are waving in the wind,
Our scarecrow comes alive!

Ryan Watkins (8)
Cwmdu School, Cwmdu

TREASURES

A dog's treasure is a mouth-watering bone,
A cat's treasure is a string ball,
A hamster's treasure is a pot of seeds,
A heron's treasure is a flapping fish,
A magpie's treasure is a flashing bottle lid,
My treasure is this poem.

Owen Silk (9)
Cwmdu School, Cwmdu

GHOST - WHAT'S THAT?

What's that whirling outside in the rain?
Only the wind and the rain down the drain.

What's that shadow on the wall over there?
Only the washing making a shadow, I swear.

What's that rattling over there on the window?
Only the wind which is making it blow.

What's that noise I can hear creaking on the floor?
Only the floorboards, I think, I'm very sure.

What's that clattering upstairs in the bathroom?
Only the clatter of a falling broom.

What's that thing I can see over there?
It can't be - can it?
It's a ghost
Aaarrgghh!

Emma Grattidge (9)
Cwmdu School, Cwmdu

POPPIES

Field of blood-red poppies,
Poppies swishing in the wind,
People who died in the war,
Poppies come from Flander's field.

Poppies in the graveyard,
To remember the war,
Remembering the dead,
Wild from Flander's field,
Rare from Flander's field.

Jonathan Hurst (10)
Forden CW Primary School, Welshpool

SNOW GOOSE

There he goes to France,
Princess too.
It is like the stars seeing the moon surrender to the sun.
I the stars, he the moon, the war the sun.
I wonder if I will ever see him again?
If he dies I do not think I could live in the
Lighthouse and look out to sea like I am now.
I could not look out at the grey damp marsh
And see all those birds.
If he comes back I will be with happiness
Once more, but if he dies I will go and live back in
The village and be sad for the rest of my life.
I can only pray now and hope that he returns.

Stephen Bolderston (10)
Forden CW Primary School, Welshpool

SNOW GOOSE POEM

White as snow, gliding through the air.
She swooped down into the reeds,
Which look like they are wrapping the whole swamp.
The snow goose scavenging for any food she can find.
She looks at the moon thinking that it is her egg.
She scales around the tower,
She knows what is happening,
Stronger than a jet she flies with the hunchback into
The forbidden world where no men go,
Guns bang as the snow goose follows into death.

George Davies (10)
Forden CW Primary School, Welshpool

YESTERDAY

Yesterday the sun blazed down, it was so hot,
We could melt into a puddle,
Today the wind is howling,
Like the wolves singing
On a silent night,
The rain is like teardrops
Splashing on
The puddles.

Today the wind is breezy,
Like the cutting cold summer.
Tree branches scrape the sky,
Grass shivers
Until all of the leaves
Fall down on the ground,
Birds swoop.

Sam Stafford (10)
Forden CW Primary School, Welshpool

SNOW GOOSE

Glides through the wind
As white as the moon
From its home in the reeded lake.
The shine of the moon
Leading on the goose's tail
As if the goose was taking the
Moon for a walk
At night he stares at the hook of a fishing rod,
Like being hypnotised.

Jake Evans (10)
Forden CW Primary School, Welshpool

CONCENTRATION CAMP

It's cold,
Strange noises of people dying,
A knock at the massive front door,
I am frightened and hungry,
People shouting,
Listen . . .
People dying.
I am thinking of my relations.
I have not a good and comfy bed, it's made of straw.
Feel angry,
The enemy might have destroyed my home.
Massive footsteps coming down the corridor,
I feel numb and lonely,
Hear the creaky front door open?
Soldiers have died for us to win the war.
Everybody thinking of the soldiers who have died.
Poppies cover the countryside to remember the soldiers.
Taking people to the shower, which killed lives.
Lonely people wanting relations.
Hear gunshots,
I am devastated.

David Roberts (9)
Forden CW Primary School, Welshpool

BLOOD-RED POPPIES

Blood-red poppies spread their wild colour
Round the countryside,
Gun shots still echo through the quiet cold sky,
Poppies pierce soft mud,
The poppies mix with the soldier's blood,
Remind us of the pain.

Joshua Gethin (9)
Forden CW Primary School, Welshpool

MAYBE PEACE

War is full of people dying,
War is full of relatives crying,
Peace makes everyone happy, not sad,
Things like peace brighten up the world,
War is dismal,
Dark and cold,
Blood spreads all over in trenches,
Peace is wonderful and clean,
When everyone is kind,
No one is mean,
War is horrible,
No matter what kind,
Peace is a lot kinder, I'm not I'll be sure you will find,
Happiness and kindness come hand in hand,
Glittering and shiny sand.

Thomas Herbert (9)
Forden CW Primary School, Welshpool

CONCENTRATION CAMP

It is dark,
I am petrified,
I feel like there is a great big hole in me
That can not connect together.
It is so cold, I feel like an icicle.
The beds are lumpy,
I wish I could escape,
But there is no way out.
I have no one to speak to.
I can hear guns blazing every minute,
I can hear people screaming and sirens wailing.

Madeleine Hughes (9)
Forden CW Primary School, Welshpool

IF I OPENED MY BOX THERE'D BE A . . . ?

Snake or a dinosaur,
Tooth or an eagle,
A piece of sugar,
Or dragon's blood,
Horn of a lizard,
Camouflaged like my toy soldiers.
An ant,
Or just a pong!
If I opened my box
There may be a leaf
Tattered and torn,
A feather floating in the box's breeze,
Or
Maybe a spider crawling
Making webs,
Waiting for the box to open
And catch a fly!

Alex Newnes (8)
Forden CW Primary School, Welshpool

THE BOX

If I opened my box there could be a silver feather
Floating up into the sky,
Or a dead worm, brown and slimy.
In the Oxo box is a rock or a bone making a clunky noise,
Maybe a pen waiting to write about a white owl
Making a night line.
A ruler waiting to draw a line
And a teddy wanting a cuddle.

Hannah Cullen-Jones (7)
Forden CW Primary School, Welshpool

WAR

War brings sadness to the nation.
Bombs pour like a landslide of death.
Deafening guns,
Like the sound of thunder
Murder.
Planes, like bees swarming
Sting.
In the graveyard dead soldiers
Rest.
Their graves mark the last wound.
The wind still blows in the poppy fields,
The rain still falls,
Tears still flow.

Shaun Williams (9)
Forden CW Primary School, Welshpool

THE WORLD OF KANDINSKY

I entered the world of Kandinsky,
Hovering on the tip of time,
Spiky stairs pointed to a jumbled universe,
Fluttering flowers were freedom's freshness,
I smelt repeating rainbow skies
And tasted breaths of midnight blue,
Gasped green, gulped yellow.
Rainbows curled and curved into waterfalls
Of reflections
Until they were boxed.
Liquorice Allsorts!

Emma Edwards (11)
Forden CW Primary School, Welshpool

MY BOX

In my box,
Maybe there's a little spider crawling around
And a snake hissing for food,
Or the seashore with a dolphin swimming and swirling,
I can hear the white ripple waves,
With the seals slicing
And wrapping wind blowing,
Streams flowing.
In my box maybe there is a train whizzing,
Cows munching waving grass
Or the daffodils blowing like a blizzard going
As the lane is captured by stones and leaves.

Sophie Howells (9)
Forden CW Primary School, Welshpool

THE BEACH

A lonely sight is the beach
at night.
The gentle lap of the waves
hitting the shore.
Seagulls scream and then settle down for the night
in their homes on the rocks.
The wind brushes across the beach
like a giant broom
tossing and turning the sand,
but never able to remove it all.
The beach is lonely maybe,
but always looking forward to the next day.

Jonathan Roberts (11)
Forden CW Primary School, Welshpool

VIKING LULLABY

Hush child, do not cry.
I will give you a sharp sword,
Sharp enough to kill monks and Saxons.

Hush child, do not cry.
I will give you a shield
To protect your love.

Hush child, do not cry.
I will give you an axe
To chop tall trees down.

Hush child, do not cry.
I will give you chainmail armour
To protect you from the enemy.

Hush child, do not cry.
You will have a longboat
To travel far and safely.

Hush child, do not cry.
I will give you a longhouse
To keep you warm and safe.

Matthew Jack Newnes (8)
Forden CW Primary School, Welshpool

THROUGH THE WINDOW

Through the window I can see lambs bleating
In the meadow and blossom trees in the wind.
Through the window I can see horses grazing in the field.
The flowing river runs by.
Through the window I can see stones rattling in the wind.
Through the window I can see my garden shed.

Alisha Gethin (8)
Forden CW Primary School, Welshpool

VIKING LULLABY

Hush child, hush.
No harm will come.
I shall protect you and give you hope.
Hush child, hush.
I shall give you strength and wisdom,
Joy and happiness
Because you, child, are ours.
You are so young and helpless
But my gifts will give you strength
To face all that is bad.
The weapons will give you power
Over war
And you will be
A person remembered for your wisdom.

Bethany Roberts (8)
Forden CW Primary School, Welshpool

CONCENTRATION CAMP

I am a nine-year-old girl living in Germany,
It is cold, not warm, no freedom,
I am so sad, scared and unhappy,
You can hear the bombing and people shouting,
Screaming and crying, crying for the loss of their families,
The soldiers are trying to find me,
You would be devastated,
People listening to the stories of the final shower,
Not to cleanse their bodies but to torture their souls,
The red of the poppy signifies the blood of the fallen heroes.

Holly Bevan (10)
Forden CW Primary School, Welshpool

THE BLOOD-STAINED WORLD

Piles of bodies burning high,
Twisting smoke in the sky,
The whirring sound of a plane,
On the horizon of the setting sun,
A blood-stained world with,
A blood-stained sky with,
A blood-stained field,
Rows of graves standing tall
And the unknown warrior proudest
Of them all.

Sam Hewitt (11)
Forden CW Primary School, Welshpool

THE SNOW GOOSE

The snow goose glides through the sky,
The wind howls,
The sea crashing on the rocks,
The boat is sailing on the water,
The lighthouse is shining on the water,
The goose is like a ghost floating in the sky,
The gun shots shooting in the distance.

Robert Anderson (9)
Forden CW Primary School, Welshpool

SEA SECRETS

Silver shells
under the calm ocean
tell tide's secret
to the strange patterned fishes.
Gleaming rainbow songs hit the bright silver rock.

Patterns tell the rainbow song that the bright silver fishes
weave bright, open the secret box.
The restless gleaming patterns tell the silver shells
not to disturb the silver unkind sharks
or they will eat you up.

Sabrina Pinchera (9)
Forden CW Primary School, Welshpool

THE WHITE CLOUD

White as blinding steam
Its golden base, sun-touched
Twirls like a helicopter
Then still as a rock
Stupid as a comedian
It slides like a clown on ice
Shaped like a doorknob
It whirls like a top
Spinning into the universe
White as blinding steam.

Benjamin Keith Roberts (10)
Forden CW Primary School, Welshpool

POPPIES

The red poppies grow
On bloody battlefields,
The blood stained the poppies to a red,
That is as red as the red, red rose.
But the smell of battle is less sweet.
It still hangs,
Full of memories.

Owen Lloyd (9)
Forden CW Primary School, Welshpool

SAD I AMS

I am . . .
An old tatty book that's never been read.
I'm put under the bed
With old junk.

I am . . .
An old broken teddy, my eyes have come off
And nobody wants me anymore.

I am . . .
An old apple tree that children climb on
And swing on and I can't spread my branches out
Because I'm scared if they break me off.

I am . . .
An old door that sometimes gets stuck.
People hit me open or kick me open.
I need to get fixed.

I am . . .
An old shoe that is tatty.
I don't know what is going on here.
They love me now they hurt me all the time.

I am . . .
An old dartboard. They bought another one.
They are all playing with him
But they never come and play with me. I'm under the stairs.

I am . . .
An old car parked
But no one wants me anymore.

I am no one
I am nothing
I am hurt by the people.

Connie Price (10)
Gelli Primary School, Pentre

THE RHONDDA

I live in the Rhondda
It's the place to be
Plenty of things to do
Plenty of things to see

The valley in the springtime
Is very lush and green
Cast your eyes around it
The prettiest sight you've seen

The river runs through the valley
The fish swim down and back
But in the days when coal was king
The river ran a dirty black

The people of the valley
Are very friendly folk
Most are kind and gentle
Who like a laugh and joke

The trees on the hillsides
The animals in the fields
Children playing in the street
This is what the Rhondda yields.

Lauren Davies (11)
Gelli Primary School, Pentre

SAD I AMS

I am a tree with branches all bare.
I am a forest empty and dark.
I am a small fly, hated, despised.
I am a peanut, rotten and smelly.
I am a warthog, ugly and wide.
I am a waste bin that's filled every day.
I am a tramp and it won't change,
Every day I wail and wail.
I want to be happy I ams,
I don't want to be *sad I ams!*

Calum Thomas (9)
Gelli Primary School, Pentre

BEAN

B   ean as thin as a pencil
E   njoys cider
A   nasty farmer
N   ever stops trying to kill Mr Fox.

Shaun Davies (8)
Gelli Primary School, Pentre

BEAN

B   ean is a smart person
E   ven he is lean like a pencil
A   lean, mean, horrible crook
N   ever stops drinking cider.

Matthew Noster (8)
Gelli Primary School, Pentre

GAGANDEEP

G agandeep is my best friend.
A mazed to have a best friend like you.
G roovy best friend, I always miss you.
A friend like you I'd never leave.
N ever be nasty to each other.
D inner together all the time.
E ach have fun and laugh.
E xtra special for you all day.
P erhaps everyone is friends like me
  And my best friend.

Jodie Matthews (9)
Gelli Primary School, Pentre

BOGGIS

B oggis, enormously fat
O ften eats chicken and dumpling pie
G oes looking out for Mr Fox
G utsy animal
I s he going to lock Mr Fox up?
S ly, horrible crook.

Phoebe Owen (8)
Gelli Primary School, Pentre

BUNCE

B unce is a small person.
U nkind and very beastly.
N asty minute *Bunce.*
C ruel little farmer.
E ven goes out hunting foxes.

Amy Jones (8)
Gelli Primary School, Pentre

SO SAD I AM

I'm,
The old book
That's never read.
I'm,
The homework sheet
Covered in black coffee.
I am,
The TV
That's never watched.

I am,
The rash
That's never itched.
I am,
The ball
That was never kicked.
I am,
The pet
That never gets fed.

I am,
The scab
That was never picked.
I am,
The CD
That doesn't play.
I am a loser.
I'm never happy.
I am no one.

Matthew Griffiths (11)
Gelli Primary School, Pentre

SAD I AMS

I am . . .
A brave warplane
Without any wings
The old pass radio
Missing my signal
The dusty book
Which no one opens.

I am . . .
The worn out shoe
Without a sole
The wobbly tooth
That's been taken away
The old rusted galleon
Missing the sail.

I am . . .
The old tank
Missing his gun
A broken down jeep
Without a wheel
The T-shirt
Without any buttons.

I am . . .
The dusty box
Cut up
The scissors
Rusted up hard to cut.

I am no good
I am no use
I am a nobody.

Jamie Fear (10)
Gelli Primary School, Pentre

SAD I AM

I am,
the chipped ruler,
have been snapped apart.
The old shoe,
without any laces.
The shirt,
That nobody likes.

I am,
an old TV
smashed to bits.
The oak tree,
having been cut down.
The gloomy old book,
having been ripped apart.

I am,
a smashed little bulb,
broken by big children.
The door,
written on by a dart.
A tooth,
that never comes out for several years.

I am,
the dusty box,
that never comes out of the attic.
The clock,
missing a number.

I am nothing important,
I am nobody,
I am never any good,
I am not respected,
I am not useful.

Tristan Foley (10)
Gelli Primary School, Pentre

FLOWERS!

Flowers along the roadside edge as wild as wild can be,
are something that I love to see but very strange to me.
Flowers in the garden that grow year by year,
are often grown by me alone, known by all to see.
Daffodils and roses, tulips and the rest,
are flowers that we see each day, I fear they're not the best.
I adore the wildest orchids, the clovers and the broom,
The scent is something special, but all are beautiful too.

Emily Farr (11)
Gelli Primary School, Pentre

BONFIRE

B onfire Night is a nice night with sparklers.
O n Bonfire Night you have barbecues.
N o one is unhappy.
F ire is hot.
I n the sky the fireworks explode.
R ed-hot flames spit out the fire.
E veryone is happy.

Georgia Macey (8)
Gelli Primary School, Pentre

GLAD I AMS

I am,
A bright little girl,
Running in the wind.
I have a mother and father,
Who are so kind
And a brother
With no mind.

I am,
Someone who's mean
And sometimes keen.
Not very clean
And could not be seen.

I am,
A little bird that lives in a tree
And sometimes
He does spells on me.
He's loving, caring, as can be.
Well I know that he,
Loves me.

I am, everything you can imagine,
I am,
I am, glad to know that you'll
Love me.

Katie Hannah Bevan (11)
Gelli Primary School, Pentre

HAPPY I AMS

I am the stars in the sky.
I am the blazing sun.
I am the lovely green grass.
I am the lovely white socks
Who are always washed.

I am the pen with lots of ink.
I am the nice piece of paper all decorated.
I am the bird with a lovely voice.
I am the lovely tree waving in the breeze.

Rebecca Wigley (10)
Gelli Primary School, Pentre

FRIENDS

F   is for friends who are fun, some people think they
    are the best in the world.
R   is for running, playing in the sunshine.
I   is for I have got a best friend, have you?
E   is for enemies sometimes become friends.
N   is for no fighting with your friends.
D   is for dinner times we eat together.
S   is for special, all your friends are the best!

Sam Rees (9)
Gelli Primary School, Pentre

BONFIRE NIGHT

In the sky I can see the bonfire crackling
And lovely multicoloured fireworks.

I can hear lots of children laughing.
I can touch food and it feels soft and nice.
I smell smoke from the bonfire.
I taste hot dogs, *mmmmmm!*

Kirsty Ward (9)
Gelli Primary School, Pentre

BUNCE

B   unce, a short nasty beast
U   nkind, scruffy, sly, crook
N   ever lets anyone eat his food
C   urled up like a ball
E   ven likes killing foxes.

Sophie McGrath (8)
Gelli Primary School, Pentre

BUNCE

B   unce, a short horrible man
U   nkind, thick animal
N   aughty, disliked crook
C   ruel, ugly, round man
E   ven becomes ill after eating doughnuts.

Rosie Davies (8)
Gelli Primary School, Pentre

BUNCE

B   unce is a dwarf farmer.
U   nkind and so hungry.
N   ever stops eating.
C   ruel and horrible man.
E   ven a mean crook.

Sophie Symons (8)
Gelli Primary School, Pentre

MY DADDO

Add some sugar and some spice,
A bit of love and care,
Some big hugs and soft kisses,
Blue eyes and a nice big smile,
Comforting hands,
Lots of things he does for me,
He makes me laugh too!

A cupful of love,
A teaspoon of care,
A heart that can never be broken,
Now my recipe
For my daddo is complete.

That's why he is special.

Danielle Taylor (11)
Gelli Primary School, Pentre

DRAGON TRAIN

D   ragons are fierce,
R   oaring along the track.
A   ll day long sleeping,
G   rouchy when woken.
O   n the track all day long.
N   o one can stop it.

T   he dragon train
R   oaring along the fields,
A   nd along the rivers.
I   n the dark tunnel,
N   ever to be seen again.

Rhys Lord (9)
Gelli Primary School, Pentre

BUNCE

B   unce, a bellied dwarf.
U   nliked farmer he kills geese.
N   asty farmer indeed.
C   ruel little beast.
E   ats doughnuts and liver all day.

Liam Evans (8)
Gelli Primary School, Pentre

BUNCE

B   unce has very sharp teeth.
U   nliked by everyone.
N   asty little dwarfed man.
C   ertainly he is very nasty.
E   very day he eats doughnuts.

Joshua Horsell (8)
Gelli Primary School, Pentre

BUNCE

B   unce is a small man
U   nkind and horrible
N   asty mean crook
C   ruel man, geese are missing
E   ats doughnuts every day.

Samantha Williams (8)
Gelli Primary School, Pentre

BOGGIS

B   oggis with an enormous fat tummy
O   ften eats chicken and dumplings
G   igantic chicken farmer
G   usty pig
I   s he going to catch him?
S   ly, very, very mean crook.

Luke Bevan (8)
Gelli Primary School, Pentre

BOGGIS

B   oggis, a mean goose farmer,
O   ften he puts chicken legs on top,
G   ets guns at night and tries to catch the fox,
G   reedy fat man,
I   s he going to catch the fox?
S   neaky old crook.

Louise Hollyman (8)
Gelli Primary School, Pentre

BUNCE

B   unce is a dwarf man
U   nkind and unpleasant
N   ever stops eating doughnuts
C   an he catch Mr Fox?
E   ven he is a fool.

Rachel Matthews (8)
Gelli Primary School, Pentre

LISTEN TO THE WIND

Listen to the wind while you're in bed.
Listen to the wind in your head.
Listen to the wind while you're in class.
Listen to the wind through the glass.
Listen to the wind while you're outside.
Listen to the wind while you've got pride.
Listen to the wind wherever you are!

Giorgia Orrells (9)
Gelli Primary School, Pentre

BOGGIS

B   oggis has a massive, fat belly.
O   n his way to find Mr Fox.
G   obble up all the chickens.
G   oose and chicken farmer.
I   nside his belly, smelly food.
S   ticky dumplings and pie he loved.

Alice Vaughan (8)
Gelli Primary School, Pentre

BOGGIS

B   oggis means nasty.
O   ften eats chickens.
G   utsy, fat and a pig.
G   oose and chicken farmer.
I   s he going to get Mr Fox?
S   ly, horrid crook.

Jorja Davies (8)
Gelli Primary School, Pentre

BONFIRE NIGHT

In the sky I can see many pretty coloured fireworks,
Blue, yellow, red, orange, turquoise, purple and pink.
I can hear lots of bangs and sizzling noises.
I touch a dead sparkler and it feels cold.
I smell hot dogs, tasty burgers and barbecues as well.
I taste hot dogs, burgers, excitement and food!

Eleanor Evans (8)
Gelli Primary School, Pentre

RACHAEL'S FAMILY

R achael is my name, yes it is.
A dam's my brother's name, Zara is my sister's.
C razy my father is, shouting, 'Wales! Go Wales!'
H urrying to Asda and forgetting her stuff is my mother for you.
A lways cooking is my nan, only for my grumpy gramps.
E ndlessly licking you is my dog, Max.
L ove never ends in my family.

Rachael Wines (10)
Gelli Primary School, Pentre

SCHOOL

S chool is funny, school is fun.
C ome along with me and have a lot of fun.
H ave some fun so come along and be a funny bee.
O h, got to go.
O n Wednesday it's choir in school.
L et's go and play a game.

Sadie Louise Jones (11)
Gelli Primary School, Pentre

SAD I AMS

I am a dustbin full of litter,
An orange a child thinks that's bitter.
I am a torn and dirty hat,
I am a ball hit by a bat.
I am a bouncy ball broken in half,
I am a cow that's just had a calf.
I am not at all important.

I am chewing gum stuck to the floor,
I am a sea horse washed onto shore.
I am a football, flat as a pancake,
I am a country struck by an earthquake.
I am a pair of shorts nobody wants to wear,
I am a barber who can't cut people's hair.
I am not important to anything.

Richard Thomas (9)
Gelli Primary School, Pentre

SAD I AMS

I am a door that is always banged.
I am a pen that's always broken.
I am a car that is always empty.
I am a book with no pages in it.
I am a teacher that always shouts.
I am a rubber that's always rubbed.

I am a bin that has never been empty.
I am a boy who is always bullied.
I am a pencil case that has been opened.
I am a balloon that's always popped.

Jamie Evans (9)
Gelli Primary School, Pentre

THE DRAGON TRAIN

T   he dragon rushing out of his lair,
H   e's looking for people to take places,
E   very day eating grass when waiting.

D   uring the night he goes to sleep.
R   oaring fire when he's
A   sleep.
G   rass is burned.
O   nly dragons breathe fire.
N   obody dares

T   o enter the cave.
R   oaring at people
A   nd
I   n a minute a red dragon comes out of a tunnel,
N   ext comes a little boy trying to catch him.

Kirsty Clayton (8)
Gelli Primary School, Pentre

DRAGON

R   aging
O   n his rock.
A   t his lair
R   oaring mad like something wild.
I   n his lava
N   ot to be felt,
G   rowling at everything that dares to come in.

Corey Dickman (8)
Gelli Primary School, Pentre

WALES FOREVER

W elsh I am living here now
A ll in a line, ready to bow
L eft here alone, all in the dark
E agles and dogs squeak and bark
S o I am a Welsh man here.

F orever more I stay still here
O ak trees blow in the deep wind
R olling a football, hurting your shin
E ver and ever growing tall
V ery thick, a stone cold wall
E very day I watch and pray
R eading a book sit and stay.

Aaron Evans (10)
Gelli Primary School, Pentre

DRAGON TRAIN

D ark and dangerous,
R oaring very loud
A long through the Tunnel of Fire,
G oing as fast as Luke Thatcher in the sports
O n the crackly, chunky track,
N othing can beat the speed of a dragon.

T errifying screams can be heard from miles away,
R ed walls from the blood of trespassers,
A n evil creature lurks inside the cave,
I have never seen it and I think
N o one has ever seen the red dragon.

Courtney Medlicott (9)
Gelli Primary School, Pentre

FRIENDS

F riends are like sisters,
R eally nice and kind,
I ce cream noses, cherry cheeks,
E mily, Lauren, that's them to a 't'.
N ever nasty, never saying no,
D elighting each other, inviting each other,
S aying sorry, saying let's be friends.

Jamie-Lee Day (9)
Gelli Primary School, Pentre

BUNCE

B unce is a pot-bellied sized dwarf.
U sed to eating doughnuts.
N ever stops eating geese all day.
C ruel, mean man.
E ven a naughty crook.

Kimberley Derham (8)
Gelli Primary School, Pentre

A RUGBY POEM

R ugby is the greatest sport, scoring a try.
U nderneath the post.
G areth Edwards is my friend.
B y far it is the best.
Y ummy food is after a good game of rugby.

Michael Adams (10)
Gelli Primary School, Pentre

SCHOOL

S   chool is one of the best things that's happened to me,
C   alling to my friends,
H   i! I say to my friends at play time,
O   n Wednesday there's choir and you sing and dance,
O   n Friday there's violin,
L   oving school is the best.

Adijana Milat (9)
Gelli Primary School, Pentre

BOGGIS

B   oggis loves eating chickens,
O   ften he eats chickens all day.
G   oes out to try and catch Mr Fox.
G   utsy Boggis has a huge tummy.
I   s he going to kill Mr Fox?
S   ly, conniving, fat crook.

Rhys Evans (8)
Gelli Primary School, Pentre

SUN

Glowing, burning,
Blazing, boiling.

Shining, scorching,
Frying, baking.

Sizzling, beautiful
Sun.

Mary-Ellen Huxter (9)
Graig-y-Wion Primary School, Pontypridd

SUN

Rising,
Appearing,
Glittering,
Shining,
Sparkling,
Burning,
Bright,
Blazing,
Fading,
Disappearing,
Gone.

Sidi Bai (8)
Graig-y-Wion Primary School, Pontypridd

GOLDEN, SHINING SUN

Golden, shining sun,
Hot, burning,
Smiling, bright,
Pretty, blushing,
Shining, sparkling sun.

Melissa Dinapoli (9)
Graig-y-Wion Primary School, Pontypridd

SUN

Singing, laughing, shining, golden,
Strong, boiling, perfect sun.
Going, going, gone,
Leaving the day.

Jenna Brooks (9)
Graig-y-Wion Primary School, Pontypridd

SUN

Boiling hot sun,
Very bright.
Big round sun
Burning.
Beautiful sun,
Glinting,
Blazing in the sky.

Rhiân Brace (9)
Graig-y-Wion Primary School, Pontypridd

SETTING SUN

Blazing bright sun,
Shining sun,
Magical,
Beautiful,
Setting sun.

Ieuan Crocker (10)
Graig-y-Wion Primary School, Pontypridd

MY HIDDEN TREASURES

I run, I climb, must keep it up, where's the treasure?
I'm lost, no map, don't know which way to the treasure.
It calls me, it is my master, where is it?
Dusk draws in, I'm breathless, still no treasure,
I sit and rest a while, I'm losing hope -
But wait - something is shining very brightly just below that cliff.
I scurry down, panting hard and there at last, I've found it,
A treasure chest full of Haribo - yes my favourite!

Bertie Jones (8)
Guilsfield CP School, Welshpool

HIDDEN TREASURE

Most people think that the graveyard
Is for the dead,
Dark grey gravestones
Mark people's heads.
Everything is quiet,
All you can hear is a cold breeze
As it stirs all the leaves.
The place is dark and desolate.

But have a closer look
At this gloomy place,
Hidden treasures everywhere
Giving so much grace.
Everything is alive,
Birds in trees, wriggly worms, bright flowers,
People with memories spending many hours.
We've found the hidden treasure.

Hannah Russell (9)
Guilsfield CP School, Welshpool

PUFFINS

I'm a puffin
Flying so high,
Looking for my supper,
A fish pie.
I look down
Upon the sea so grey,
Where upon
I see my prey -
Hidden treasure.

Jackson Lee-Jones (8)
Guilsfield CP School, Welshpool

THE SILENCE

Quiet! The war goes on,
My voice will break the silence,
The sound rings out,
It looks like fire waves,
It melts and burns everything in its path,
Coming in lower and lower the planes fly,
They can't miss,
They hit my bomb shelter,
My life ends now!
Screaming, shouting all around me,
I fall into the gates of Hell.
Ice-cold hands all over my body,
Pulling me down into the whirlpool of death!
Down, down I go into the fiery depths of Hell,
The Devil is near!

Helen Morgan (10)
Guilsfield CP School, Welshpool

ANIMALS

A   newborn animal is always cute,
N   o animal I don't like,
I   t is great to have a pet of your own,
M   y pet is a rabbit,
A   nimals live in the wild and in your home,
L   oads of animals live on the Earth,
S   ea creatures such as dolphins, fish and sharks.

There are animals that live in the jungle, like snakes and tigers.
There are animals that live in hot countries, like cheetahs and elephants.
There are animals that live in your home and your garden, like dogs,
cats and rabbits.

Lyndsey Jones (11)
Guilsfield CP School, Welshpool

HELL

You get pulled through
The fiery gates of Hell,
As you land
The pain fights through your body,
I see the devils guarding
The forbidding castle of death.
As I walk closer and closer,
They glare at me
With their big, red, gleaming eyes,
As I step inside the forbidding castle,
I see souls
And at the top is the Devil,
Guarded by a pair of Dementors
That suck your soul,
I cry out loud,
'Help!'

Lynzee-Kim Sinden (10)
Guilsfield CP School, Welshpool

ANIMAL WOOD

As you're walking through the wood when the leaves blow,
A silent rustling of the grass,
There are badgers, rabbits, all sorts of creatures
And if I could talk to the animals and read their little minds,
I'd be having fun right now in a burrow or a hive.
Don't you see how cute they are as they scamper through the wood?
Down underneath the rose bush in the slippery slime
Lies a big round hedgehog curled up in its bed.
There's a hare with her babies beside her
And a father round the back.
So I wish I could talk to the animals and read their little minds.

Jessica Thomas (8)
Guilsfield CP School, Welshpool

HIDDEN TREASURES

'Twas windy when I started,
My journey for the dodo.
The rain was whipping through the sky
Like bubbles in the water.
There was me and the cook
And the captain's crew
And the mate of the good ship Rose.

Every day was much the same,
Dark, desolate and empty.
No creatures bred on this land,
The gloom was immense.
No cattle lived on these strange acres -
Well, they wouldn't - it was sea!

Even after meals we didn't feel too well,
So I went to do my duty
And leant over the boat.
When I'd done
I looked upwards at the turquoise sky
And what a wondrous sight was that,
That therefore met my eye,
A bird with a morsel in its mouth,
Land, oh land ahoy.
Hurrah, hurrah, oh what a brilliant day,
For land it was, oh boy it was
And then I saw waddle forwards
The lost dodo heading south.

And now I look back on those days
Of excitement, sadness and woe,
The only tale I ever tell is the tale,
Of the dodo.

Bethany Wilcox (9)
Guilsfield CP School, Welshpool

A TRIP INTO SPACE

A rocket came to my front door,
One night on Christmas Eve,
I went to the door and they told me that I would receive,
A pocketful of sweets,
I took up all the seats,
And then I saw some little men,
Coming in huge fleets.
There were about 100
That shows how small they were.

Then one great big alien stood up to say,
'I am sure young boy, you will get good pay,
Just come with us now and help me.'
Then he walked off in a funny sort of way,
We blasted off into space
And I saw the moon's face.

It is amazing up here, up around the stars,
I saw a red planet, it looks just like Mars.
Then we stopped on a yellowish planet,
I stood on the ground, it felt squishy,
It is true, the moon is made out of cheese,
After I had eaten as much as possible, we left.

We made for their home, I was full up with cheese,
We landed on the planet,
There was no sign of any trees,
I then took out some seeds,
From the inside of my pocket,
And out grew lovely trees,
In reward, they gave me a diamond locket.
Before I left, they took me to the Millennium Dome,
Then straight away, they took me back home.

Lucy Gwilt ((11)
Guilsfield CP School, Welshpool

THE APPLE

Apples are round
Apples are red
They fill you up
Before you go to bed!

Apples are fat
Apples are green
They are a big
Mean, fighting machine!

Apples are round
Apples are red
Apples are green
We all like them
Because they're shiny and clean
Apples!

Jade Griffiths (10)
Guilsfield CP School, Welshpool

HIDDEN TREASURES

The ship was rocking against the rocks,
Water was crashing and splashing,
The waves were big,
All of a sudden it calmed down.
We all saw a little fin,
A little bottlenose dolphin popped up,
I spoke, he spoke back.
The waves were going over the top of him.
He said, 'I must go and find my friends.'
His coat was sleek.
He swam back gracefully.

Katie Davies (8)
Guilsfield CP School, Welshpool

WHY DOES EVERYONE BLAME IT ON ME?

Why me?
Why me?

Why does everyone blame it on me?
I don't always do this
I don't always do that.
I might do it on my own
But it's not always me, if I'm not alone.
Why does everyone blame it on me?

A shout across the classroom
When it's not even me.
Why does everyone blame it on me?
Someone falls over in games,
Who's always blamed?
Me!

Beverley Lloyd (10)
Guilsfield CP School, Welshpool

FOOD

I love to eat Mum's chips,
Lots of salt and vinegar too.
They're thick and chunky but soft inside
Which means I don't have to chew.
A nice big slice of pizza
With tasty tomato and cheese.
Mum knows my next question will be,
'Any more please?'
It's ice cream and jelly for pudding,
I hope it's raspberry ripple.
And then I think I'll have apple juice
As it's just my favourite tipple.

Katie Gittins (9)
Guilsfield CP School, Welshpool

THE MAD SCIENTIST

The attic was very spooky and dark,
A man was working on an amazing machine,
We went up to him,
He was mad,
Red faced and hair on end,
He turned us tiny,
Just one press of a button,
Ohhh!
It doesn't make anything big.

'I'll try to make you return to normal,
Go and get me a pound of treasure.'
Under that ancient floorboards
Dark and damp,
We found the pound of gold,
It was very gold and bright.

He turned us back,
We never went in that attic again.

James Hatton (9)
Guilsfield CP School, Welshpool

ONE DAY I TRAVELLED INTO SPACE

One day I travelled into space
To see the first of the alien race.
They had green skin
And red stubby toes
And one had a sparkly nose.

One day I travelled into space
To see the first of the alien race.
Their UFOs are very bright
And don't look exactly right.

One day I travelled into space
To see the first of the alien race.
The leader was big and fat
And he had a very nice mat,
But I couldn't see a single cat.

One day I travelled into space
To see the last of the alien race.
No green skin,
Or red stubby toes
And I can't see the sparkly nose.

Philip White (10)
Guilsfield CP School, Welshpool

THE SCHOOL

The school is a happy place,
Everybody likes to race.
We start the school day at 9am,
But just before school starts, we play a game.
At playtime, we run around . . .
In the playground.

We go into our lessons,
English, maths or PE.
I look around and see
Robbie climbing a tree.

So that is my school,
It's not very cool . . .
But I like it.

Matthew Jones (10)
Guilsfield CP School, Welshpool

MY HIDDEN TREASURES

I've never seen a robin before.
Robins can fly.
They come out at Christmas.
They look nice in a picture full of snow.
They have a red chest.
They have different brown wings.
They eat worms.
Robins can see other birds in the sky.
Robins fly everywhere.
There are lots of robins.
Some robins go on house roofs.
Robins like sunshine.
Robins like children,
And robins make a really good nest in tall silver trees.
Robins don't like noisy cars, lorries or vans.
Robins like the moon and stars,
And robins like the big school.
Robins can see lots of people in this school.
Robins find other robins in the sky
And they play a game in the sky,
They play at catching other birds.

Richelle Griffin (8)
Guilsfield CP School, Welshpool

FEELINGS

Happy is joyful,
It smells like candy,
It is the colour pink,
It is like a pink pillow.

Sad is upsetting,
It smells like smelly socks,
It is the colour grey,
It is like raw potato.

Love is happy,
It smells like honeysuckle,
It is the colour red,
It is like a red rose.

Loneliness is scary,
It smells like a dark, empty wood,
It is the colour black,
It is like a brick wall.

Emma Graham (10)
Guilsfield CP School, Welshpool

CHOCOLATE CAKES

Chocolate is yummy
For everyone's tummy.
You eat it every day,
Even when you play.
When it's any time of year
You eat it with loads of wine and beer.
You put it in when you make cakes
To make it scrummy when it bakes.

I love it, love it, love it,
Not just a bit.
All my friends love it when they play,
They eat it like me every day.
Cakes, I love them with chocolate on,
I love them with chocolate in.
I love it, love it, love it.

Chocolate cakes!

Emma Davies (10)
Guilsfield CP School, Welshpool

HIDDEN TREASURES

My christening was over
And now we were going home
To open my presents.
My first present was a statue of the Millennium Dome.
The best gift was the chest,
On the lid it had golden fancy writing saying, *My Treasures.*
Also I had a vest with a jest on it.
When I was six we moved house,
And my mistake was to leave the chest behind . . .

When I was twenty-nine
My father was ill, his name was really Bill.
One day my mum came and told me about the chest,
So a week later I decided to go and find the chest.
I was still twenty-nine . . .
There I was standing in front of the front door,
I could see the sign, *Orchard House.*
Finally I was in the gloomy and dusty attic,
I could just see a bare box,
Inside was the chest. I opened the chest
And found my treasures but before I shut the chest
I saw a glow so I peered down,
And I found it was the rarest diamond ring.

Lowri Evans (8)
Guilsfield CP School, Welshpool

THE FRUIT BOWL

Inside, a small plum, red and shiny,
Also I see a juicy orange like the sun,
I think I see a pack of grapes, oval and green.

A shiny red apple looking at me,
I see a yellow banana poking out,
All this fruit is making me hungry.

I think I shall have some,
I'd better ask Mum.
Oh I do need something to fill my tum,
That fruit does look yum!

Philip Hughes (11)
Guilsfield CP School, Welshpool

MY BEST FRIENDS

Rachel is my best friend because she makes me laugh
At the things she says and does,
She helps me with my work
And she comes to my house every three weeks,
We always have a midnight feast,
Rachel is my best friend ever,
She plays computer games
And she is really good at them.

Kelly is my best friend because she makes me laugh
And has fun whenever I am sad,
She always comes up to me
And asks me what is the matter.
Kelly is kind and helps you up
Whenever you are hurt.
She likes music,
Kelly is a good friend to have about.

Rhianonn is my best friend because
She makes me laugh underneath.
She has lots and lots of fun.

All of these are my best friends.

Laura Mary Sinclair (11)
Guilsfield CP School, Welshpool

ME

It sparkled, glinting in the light,
Blinking and seeing everything,
Trees, grass, a grey and a green,
The eye, the onlooker.

It stretched, grasping the object,
Slipping and sliding,
Gripping and grasping,
The hand, the helper.

It raced, swallowing the object,
Flattening the green,
It thuds, crashing down,
The foot, the supporter.

Higher and higher,
Blocking the light,
Stretching, getting dangerously higher . . .
The arm, the robot.

They bend, leap and jump,
Twirling and swirling,
They collapse, exhausted,
The legs, the traveller.

It opens wide,
Red and glistening white,
They bite and snap,
The mouth, the talker.

It shouts and screams,
The supreme leader,
Dull and grey, not pretty,
The brain, the master.

I am a work of art in myself,
Me, the king of them all.

Madeleine Carver (10)
Guilsfield CP School, Welshpool

HIDDEN TREASURES

I'm going on an adventure,
I'm going where I've never been before.
What am I going to find?
What's that up ahead?
I can see golden yellow, shimmering sprinkles,
Looks like a beautiful beach.
It is, it's a secret beach, I've found some treasure,
Look at the clean, soft sand, look at the lovely blue sea,
What are those two birds?
The sand is so clean,
Oh no I can see a storm coming,
The waves are crashing,
They're smashing,
They're lashing,
It's a tidal wave,
'Aaaaahhhh!'
I . . . I'm still alive,
I think it's time to go home,
But my boat is smashed.
'Help! Help!' I can see another boat.
'In you come I'll take you home.'

Laura Speake (9)
Guilsfield CP School, Welshpool

WHY ME?

Why is it always me who gets the blame?
I shouldn't be the one ashamed.
I might do some things
But I don't do them all,
Why is it always me?

Why is it always me who gets blamed?
I shouldn't be the one ashamed,
When we have an argument
Chatting at the table
Why is it always me?

Why is it always me who gets the blame?
I shouldn't be the one ashamed,
When we are fighting in the playground,
About a silly goal,
Why is it always *me?*

Abbie Gittins (11)
Guilsfield CP School, Welshpool

BEST FRIENDS

Best friends are very special,
They make you laugh,
They make you very happy.
Ciara is my best friend,
Along with all my other friends
She is so special in every way,
She makes me happy every day,
She comes to my house and we will play
Lots of games together,
We will be friends forever together.

Jennifer Morgan (10)
Guilsfield CP School, Welshpool

BUSY STREETS OF LONDON

Running round London, it's busy, busy, busy
in and out of shops with my best friend Izzy
Spending lots, Izzy's getting dizzy.
In and out of traffic, I am beeping my horn
life is going on, don't wanna be born.
There's a man on the pavement singing a rap
and all he has to eat is a mouldy burger bap.
Went into a supermarket to get a chicken curry
lots of people barged in and there was a robbery.
Finally, I went home sitting on the couch
I went to get my curry out of my front pouch
I put it in the microwave, it's boiling hot,
got some salt and pepper and shoved
it all in a pot.

Joel William Dyos (11)
Guilsfield CP School, Welshpool

HIDDEN TREASURES

S omething special in my room,
O ften I read them when I'm full of gloom.
P utting my feet up
H igh on my bouncy bed,
I nteresting stories,
E verlasting stories.

B right new books belonging to me.
O ver and over,
O ver again,
K eep reading and reading my
S ophie books.

Sophie Bough (9)
Guilsfield CP School, Welshpool

THE JOURNEY

I was lonely in the middle of a desert,
No one around for miles and miles.
Not a tree in sight,
Not a plane in flight,
Not even a fence with stiles.

So I walked on and on,
I couldn't see an oasis.
I started to run,
I had lots of fun,
But I didn't see any faces.

I came to a dark, dark wood,
There was a smell which was foul.
I looked to the sky,
I don't quite know why,
But then I saw a brown owl.

I heard the noise of a rushing river,
I didn't hear anything else at all.
It couldn't be far
My mum left her car,
Right next to a waterfall.

I came to the end of my adventure,
I came to the end of my journey.
I was a long time,
But it isn't a crime,
That my mum was in a great fury!

Jenny Lewis (10)
Guilsfield CP School, Welshpool

ANIMALS

Deers jumping, frogs croaking,
Fish swimming, birds humming,
Dogs barking, cats miaowing,
Animals everywhere.

Butterflies fluttering, sharks hunting,
Caterpillars munching, crabs pinching,
Shrimps crawling, snails sliding,
Animals everywhere.

Foxes lurking, moles digging
Badgers sleeping, worms wriggling,
Woodlice eating, ants biting,
Animals everywhere.

Rabbits hopping, camels resting,
Guinea pigs roaming, hamsters playing,
Gerbils eating, owls hooting,
Animals everywhere.

Rats scampering, mice squeaking,
Whales splashing, dolphins jumping,
Snakes hissing, spiders crawling,
Animals everywhere.

Pigs snorting, horses galloping,
Monkeys swinging, elephants playing,
Lizards sunbathing, bees stinging,
Animals everywhere.

Rhiannon Jones (10)
Guilsfield CP School, Welshpool

HIDDEN TREASURE

I'm sitting in my room locked away,
I haven't had breakfast, dinner or tea,
Reading fantastic Famous Five books,
Book after book
As if I've never read before!
But I'm scared,
I haven't been to school or had any play,
All I hear is *bang, bang!* all day and night,
But I don't care because I'm locked in my room
Away from everybody,
Reading Famous Five books.
I don't care if people make fun of me!
I don't care about anything as long as I'm reading,
Because it's all about me,
It's treasure to me!
They don't know it, it's treasure to me.
Not to them, they have got dogs and cats to play with,
I haven't got an animal at all,
So I read, read, read, more and more
Of the Famous Five!
And I'm happy reading all alone.
I don't watch TV now like I used to!
All I do is read all day!
It's been two months and I've read fifteen books and I've got two left.
Now I have to get another book to read.

Jennie Morris (9)
Guilsfield CP School, Welshpool

THE BANANA

The banana is long and bendy
And very, very friendly,
It looks like my aunty Wendy,
Because her hair is yellow and trendy.

Its friends are orange and pink
And tastes good when it flavours a drink,
You should feed your bulging tummy,
Because bananas are very, very yummy.

We grow on trees,
In hot coun-ter-ies,
We grow as a hand,
In time we expand.

By the natives we are picked,
Into the crates we are clicked,
There's a long journey ahead,
'Where're the bananas?' everyone said.

Lucy Davies (11)
Guilsfield CP School, Welshpool

KENNING - DOG

Tail wagger,
Paw licker,
Cat chaser,
Bone finder,
Mat sleeper,
Bone beggar,
Ball chaser,
Love seeker.

James Morgan (10)
Hirwaun Primary School, Aberdare

KENNINGS - FOOTBALL

Net buster,
Ball dribbler,
Air puncher,
Wild diver,
Ball slammer,
Loud shouter,
Goal scorer,
Ball saver,
Long thrower,
Powerful header,
Tactics maker,
Foul commiter,
Penalty shooter,
Hand shaker,
Shirt swapper,
Big defender,
Championship winner.

Benjamin Duckham (11)
Hirwaun Primary School, Aberdare

HORSE

Ears pointed
Eyes glaring
Muzzle snorting
Teeth grinding
Head tossing
Mane flickering
Coat gleaming
Tail swishing
Legs pawing
Hoofs clattering

Samantha Maria Elias (10)
Hirwaun Primary School, Aberdare

KENNING'S DOG

Paw licker
Bone chewer
Tail wagger
Fun lover
Ball chewer
Child chaser
Ear nibbler
Water slurper
Loud burper
Fast runner
Slipper ripper
He's always barking
You'll never change him
He's my dog.

Rhys Jones (11)
Hirwaun Primary School, Aberdare

MY MAD CAT

My mad cat
Is as big as a tree,
My mad cat
Is as clever as me.
She follows me round
Wherever I go,
When she lies down
She fills all the floor.
She drinks from the tap
When she wants water,
She does this
Because my father taught her.

Stacey Louise Kerr (11)
Hirwaun Primary School, Aberdare

THE BLUE WORLD OF DANGER AND FANTASY

Deep, deep down under the sea,
There is a magical world of
Fantasy
Where mermaids swim
And dolphins wander.
An octopus guards Neptune's treasure
But deeper down, there's danger lurking.
Grey sharks glide smoothly past
Their white eyes watching, working
Through the gloomy water, ready
To pounce on a fishy victim.
Back up we go
Into the light
Where colourful coral
Gives shelter to many different fish.
A beautiful sea horse clings onto some weed
Moving back and forth in the gentle current
Peaceful and tranquil, there's nowhere quite like it.
How I wish I could live in the wonderful
Ocean.

Alicia Ewington (9)
Hirwaun Primary School, Aberdare

MY WALK

I was out one day on a walk,
When I saw my friend, we started to talk,
All of a sudden it turned so cold,
James shouted and sounded so bold.
Then I started to make my way home,
As I got near my mother shouted,
'There's someone on the phone!'

Corey Addiscott (10)
Hirwaun Primary School, Aberdare

KENNING'S DOG

Tail flicker
   Loud barker
      Fur licker
         Great growler
            Fast runner
               Cat chaser
            Flea scratcher
         Postman scarer
      Bone chewer
   Face licker
Park walker
   Sloppy kisser
      Stick fetcher
         Slipper bringer
            Fireside lounger
               Farm helper
            Home guarder
         Sled puller
      Fox hunter
   Race winner
Blind helper.

Man's best friend!

Stephanie Abraham (9)
Hirwaun Primary School, Aberdare

UNDER THE OCEAN

Drifting I saw a sea horse as shiny as pearls,
Gliding I touched a mermaid as soft as pillows,
Sinking I tasted salt as salty as popcorn,
Floating I felt as light as a feather.

Lorren Daily (11)
Hirwaun Primary School, Aberdare

KENNINGS - DOGS

Bone cruncher,
Cat chaser,
Hole digger,
Farm worker,
Ball chaser,
Fox hunter,
Crime cater,
Best friend,
Wet nose,
Keen smell,
House guarder,
Wood chewer,
Car racer,
Drugs finder,
Blind man's eyes,
People rescuer,
Circus performer,
Sledge puller.

Samantha Brookman (10)
Hirwaun Primary School, Aberdare

HIDDEN TREASURE

Hidden treasures are your pets,
Hidden treasures are your warm-hearted memories,
Hidden treasures are your loving family,
Hidden treasures keep you safe,
Hidden treasures are your love you can't buy,
Love anywhere with your photographs
You can see when you are little.
Hidden treasure is a pot of gold but who
Cares about gold, when you have love and care.

Benjamin Barnett (9)
Hirwaun Primary School, Aberdare

SATURDAY FOOTBALL

It's Saturday morning, I'm worried today,
The under-11s are about to play.
We pay our pound at the YMCA,
Squeeze into cars and we're on our way.
The rain had made the ground really soggy,
The mud was thick and the goalmouth boggy.
I tackled a boy twice the size of me,
My best friend Dan got kicked on the knee,
At half-time we all stopped for rest,
Our fans kept calling, 'Hirwaun are the best!'
The final whistle blows, we're 3-0 up,
I think we might just win the cup.
When I arrived home lunch was waiting for me,
I still can't forget Dan's poor old knee.

James Shilton (10)
Hirwaun Primary School, Aberdare

KENNING - CAT

Tail waver,
Mouse chaser,
Fish eater,
Night creeper,
Basket sleeper,
Bird scratcher,
Quiet purrer,
Paw licker,
Eye flicker,
Water hater,
Whisker tickler.

Lauren Lewis (10)
Hirwaun Primary School, Aberdare

BURIED TREASURE

Treasure is something longing to be found,
It is something often found underground,
Treasure is something put there for a cause,
So watch out, it might be someone's toes or someone's nose!
Treasure lies on the seabed,
Or it could appear anywhere,
But one thing's for sure, you'll never find
Some in your knicker drawer!

Sea divers often find it
Anywhere you can think,
So next time you go swimming, remember to take your goggles
And a snorkel, to try and find a link!

It's a shame fish don't find treasure,
Next time you see a fish there's no point looking
Because they laze about in leisure!
Sometimes treasure is something you can see,
But don't bother looking, just go back to your cup of tea!
Sometimes it's luck you can feel,
But how can you be sure it's not just an eel!
Treasure is something longing to be found,
It is often found underground,
Treasure is something put there for a cause,
So watch out, it could be someone's toes, or someone's nose!

Ashlee Evans (10)
Hirwaun Primary School, Aberdare

DAVID GHOUL AND HIS BEAR

There was a man from Blackpool,
Who's name was David Ghoul
And he had a bear
Which he treated really unfair,
Then David died in a swimming pool.

But the story doesn't end there,
For the bear drank some beer
And got very drunk,
So he put on a pair of swimming trunks,
From then on the bear's name was Mr Bunks.

Martyn Thomas Bell (11)
Hirwaun Primary School, Aberdare

BOOKS

If you want at your own leisure,
You can hunt for buried treasure,
For lots of fun that you can't measure,
All inside a book,
Open up the dusty pages,
Different characters, different ages,
Peter Pan, Captain Hook,
Fun, all inside a book.

Dominic Silva (11)
Hirwaun Primary School, Aberdare

THE FOUR SEASONS

Snowdrop, snowdrop on the ground,
Spring is coming all around,
Blossoms growing on the trees,
Extra pollen for the bees.
Autumn is here, leaves turn brown,
Watch them all come tumbling down,
Now snow is falling thick and fast,
I've built a snowman, how long will he last?

Sara Busby (10)
Hirwaun Primary School, Aberdare

THE SEA!

The sea is as cold as ice,
It whooshes and it washes,
As it cools my feet it's nice,
As the sand drifts in.

The shells are washed ashore,
I see at the corner of my eye,
A treasure chest hidden inside a cave,
I go to have a peep but what can I hear?
My mum calling me for an ice cream.

I run over to her with excitement,
We walk to the shop,
I ask the lady for a double strawberry ice cream
And we both leave to go home.

Rebecca Jayne Wilkins (11)
Hirwaun Primary School, Aberdare

KENNING - DOG

Face licker,
Cat catcher,
Tail wagger,
People lover,
Slipper eater,
Bone cruncher,
Postman hater,
House wetter,
Sun liker,
Rain hater.

Laura Davies (10)
Hirwaun Primary School, Aberdare

HIDDEN TREASURES

A hidden treasure is a secret of life,
A hidden treasure is something you keep,
If you keep it all your life,
It will stay there very deep,
A memory of you and your friends years ago,
A memory of you and your family at home,
A hidden treasure will stay safe like a dome.

Selina May David (9)
Hirwaun Primary School, Aberdare

HIDDEN TREASURES

Gold, silver, bronze and money,
You don't need them all,
Gold, silver, bronze and money,
Can't give you love and care.
Family and friends can give you love and care
And a safe home is all you need to keep
Your treasures locked up.

Emily Jones (9)
Hirwaun Primary School, Aberdare

UNDER THE SEA

Sinking I saw a mermaid as colourful as a rainbow,
Gliding I touched a dolphin smooth as silk,
Floating I tasted seaweed as salty as chips,
Splashing I felt as heavy as a rock.

Michaela Pedro (10)
Hirwaun Primary School, Aberdare

KENNING - DOG

Tail wagger,
Water dribbler,
Meat eater,
Toy player,
People lover,
Good swimmer,
Cat chaser,
Extreme runner,
Loud barker.

John Mullaney (10)
Hirwaun Primary School, Aberdare

KENNING - DRAGON

Skin ripper,
Bone cruncher,
Fire breather,
Knight fighter,
Man eater,
Claw scratcher,
Wing flapper.

James Smith (10)
Hirwaun Primary School, Aberdare

HIDDEN TREASURE

Gold and silver are treasure,
So are family and friends,
Rubies and bronze are treasure,
So is love and care.

Treasure can be special
And treasure can not,
But I like a home to stay in
But you might not.

Ellisha Nadine Hughes (8)
Hirwaun Primary School, Aberdare

MY RATS

My rats are very unusual
And a bit clumsy too.

My favourite one is Tinker
Who likes to find you.

Scank is the one which
Always tries something new.

I like my rats and so should you.

Fenn Moss-Izzard (11)
Hirwaun Primary School, Aberdare

HIDDEN TREASURES

Hidden treasures are loving families,
Hidden treasures are loyal friends
And good memories,
Hidden treasures make you smile,
Because you can't travel back in time,
Old photos make you laugh,
To remind you that you have a warm heart.

Natasha Eynon (9)
Hirwaun Primary School, Aberdare

THE COUNTRYSIDE

T he countryside is the most beautiful thing in the world,
H edges have animals living in them like hedgehogs and rabbits,
E very bird sings a delightful tune in the countryside.

C ows graze in the lush green fields,
O n the mountainside lambs bounce joyfully in the long summer day,
U nder the big bushy trees, sheep lie in the shade,
N obody should ever harm the countryside, we must care for
    it for tomorrow
T he rabbit freezes as he sees the fox lurking near him,
R oads are dangerous for all creatures.
Y ears go by but the countryside never changes, it is always beautiful,
S ummer is a happy season for all living creatures,
I ce drives the birds south for the winter months,
D own in the countryside creatures come alive,
E ven though some animals are predators, I think we shouldn't
    harm them.

Rachel Perry (10)
Libanus CP School, Brecon

COUNTRYSIDE

In the morning,
I hear the birds singing their tunes.

I can hear the great, big storm,
Whooshing through the trees.

In the countryside, I can touch
The rough bark.

I feel the sharp twigs and smooth green leaves.

Harry Lowles (8)
Libanus CP School, Brecon

RUN, RABBIT, RUN

The rabbit is running over hills and mountains,
But what's he running from?
Leaps over streams and rushing rivers,
But what's he running from?
Racing against mysterious winds,
But what's he running from?
Springs over stones and dusty rocks,
But what's he running from?
Sprints and weaves through bushes and grass,
But what's he running from?
Stops, panting in front of a murky lake,
But what's he running from?
No time to stop, he jumps right in,
What's he running from?
Swimming, panting with all his might,
What's he running from?

Jenny Jones (11)
Libanus CP School, Brecon

THE COUNTRYSIDE

In the countryside, I see the river flowing,
Its soft, smooth water runs slowly by,
Go close and touch the countryside river.

In the countryside, I see the birds flying,
Their soft voices whistling smoothly through my ears.

In the countryside, I see the clouds swooping in the sky,
The sound of nothing but peace,
They look so soft and smooth,
In the countryside.

Mariah Chapman (9)
Libanus CP School, Brecon

THE COUNTRYSIDE

In the countryside I smell lush green grass
And then damp leaves rotting in the wood.
As I walk through the garden, I smell the freshly cut grass
And the flowers sweet smell slowly flows up my nose.

In the countryside I hear the birds' soft songs and the
Rustling sturdy trees,
Then the rain comes and I hear the rain hitting the ground
With a thump and a bump and the water dripping through
The leaves,
I can hear the wind blowing like a giant's breath.

In the countryside I can feel the rough bark on the giant trees
And the soft silky petals of the wild woodland flowers,
I can feel the woolly sheeps' fur flowing through my fingers
And the nettles plucking at my hands.

In the countryside I can taste fresh new vegetables
And creamy warm milk slipping right down my throat.

In the countryside I can see the great mountains as high as the sky
And the lazy sheep grazing the lush green grass,
I see birds zi zagging through the sky like jets,
In the countryside.

Luke Jackson (11)
Libanus CP School, Brecon

COUNTRYSIDE

In the countryside,
I can see the swaying trees like dark black figures,
Standing straight and tall.

In the countryside,
I can see the hot, yellow, red and orange sun
Hanging in the sky shining down on me.

In the countryside,
I can see and smell the blossoming red roses
And tulips.

In the countryside,
I touch the pink, soft
Rose petals as soft as velvet.

Emma Samuel (9)
Libanus CP School, Brecon

THE COUNTRYSIDE

In the countryside,
I can smell fresh air -
As fresh as the clean sheets that have just come off
The washing line
And fresh breezes that blow as cold as ice.

In the countryside,
I can see the bright yellow, red and orange
Sun warming our land
And the dark green mountains with green
And brown trees growing.

In the countryside,
I can taste the cows snow-white milk
And juicy berries picked from the hedgerows.

In the countryside,
I can touch the orange autumn leaves
And the rough bark on the tall trees.

In the countryside,
I can hear the trees as they blow side to side,
I can hear smooth breezes blowing.

Katie Jones (9)
Libanus CP School, Brecon

THE COUNTRYSIDE

In the countryside,
I can see, hear, feel, taste and smell,

I see the birds playing in the breeze,
I see the trees start to sway and sway,
I see the sun that is like a glistening ball,
It looks like it's going to stay all day.

I hear the birds happily singing a sweet song
And the sheep eating the grass with
The munching of their mouths
Sounding like grinding machines.

I can feel the grass
And the bark on the trees,
I feel the fresh spring breeze
Blowing on my face.

I smell the roses
And the sweet smell of summer,
I smell the fresh morning dew
On the ground.

In the countryside,
I taste the air
And the fresh water that's lovely and cold,
I taste the smell of spring,
Welcoming a new season.

Jessica Holroyd (10)
Libanus CP School, Brecon

BONFIRE NIGHT

Boom!
Bang!
Colours!
Glowing green and red flames,
Booming blues, they shoot up smoothly
Through the black sky,
Everyone is shouting,
Screaming,
Wailing,
All the fireworks dazzling in the black alleyway sky,
The babies start crying,
Suddenly it starts again,
Like it's a war zone,
Pretty colours of the bonfire,
Light amber,
Sunny yellow,
Dark red,
You see the puppet of Guy Fawkes,
Melting like a candle,
People happy,
Waving sparklers,
They watch the fireworks with a glow in their eyes,
Then after the show, it's time to go,
The ashes fade,
The smoke finally disappears,
The bonfire goes out!

Ben Miles (9)
Llanfaes Community Primary School, Brecon

BONFIRE NIGHT

The night like a deep black ocean,
Catherine wheels screaming like sirens,
Bonfire roaring,
Volcanoes emptying,
Bonfire blazing, a scorching sun,
Fireworks shooting rapidly into the air,
Colours explode,
Gleaming greens,
Raging reds,
Sizzling hot dogs,
People munching,
Fantastic display,
Kids cheering,
Then!
The water kills the flames
And the smoke drifts away.

Alexander Griffiths (9)
Llanfaes Community Primary School, Brecon

TEN THINGS FOUND IN A WIZARD'S POCKET

A big purple hat,
A bit of magic dust,
Some spell books,
A little slimy frog,
A flying broomstick,
Some squeaky mice,
A shiny wand,
Some magic paper,
A brown and white owl,
A blue velvet rabbit.

Maxine Davies (7)
Llanfaes Community Primary School, Brecon

PRECIOUS STONES

Bloodstones,
Bloodstone red like the blood in my veins.
Diamonds,
Diamonds glowing like the sun.
Pearls,
Pearls gleam like eyes.
Rubies,
Ruby raindrops.
Opal,
Opals cloud white.
Amber,
Amber as yellow sunset.
Sapphire,
Sapphire blue skies and turquoise grass.
Amethyst,
Amethyst as bright as fireworks.

Thomas Price (9)
Llanfaes Community Primary School, Brecon

PRECIOUS STONES

Diamonds,
Glittering in the golden sun.
Rubies,
Reflecting like a shining mirror of liquid mist.
Sapphire,
Like big dancing raindrops.
Amber,
Like a hot golden desert of melting sand.
Opal,
Like the bright light of the moon.

Cameron Gardner (10)
Llanfaes Community Primary School, Brecon

BONFIRE NIGHT

Whoosh!
Fireworks dazzle in the sea of black,
Roaring red,
Blazing blue,
Growling green!

The bonfire rips at the empty darkness,
Flashing rockets rage against the dark night,
Splashing sparks spit from roaring Roman candles,
Spinning Catherine wheels blaze like a maddening fair ride,
As the guy is hurled upon the blazing mountain of flame,
He melts like chocolate in a fierce sun,
Then the fire dies and is left in slumber,
While everyone walks away looking forward to next year
And the smoke drifts up to die in the darkness.

Stephen Gibson (9)
Llanfaes Community Primary School, Brecon

TEN THINGS FOUND IN A WIZARD'S POCKET

Some golden money,
A dusty wand,
A red feather,
Some old pens,
An old dusty book,
Some false teeth,
An ancient map,
Some magic dust,
Some scary spiders,
A horrible broomstick.

Lisa Foster (7)
Llanfaes Community Primary School, Brecon

PRECIOUS STONES

A diamond,
Bright sunshine on a hot summer's day,
An opal,
Gleaming in the ancient ground lying there forever,
Pearls,
Black dark like the silent night,
Rubies,
Trembling like the morning sun,
Bloodstones,
Bright dripping like red rain,
Colourless moonstone,
Invisible white ghosts in the night,
Sapphires,
Delicate in the wind,
The amber reflecting rainbows of colour.

Iwan Rees (10)
Llanfaes Community Primary School, Brecon

TEN THINGS FOUND IN A WIZARD'S POCKET

A big dragon,
Some shining stones,
A furry owl,
An old spell book shining in the sun,
Some false teeth,
A shiny wand glittering in sun,
Some squeaking mice,
Some golden money,
A magical dog,
A glass feather.

Jessica Jones (7)
Llanfaes Community Primary School, Brecon

PRECIOUS STONES

Amber,
Like the dying yellow sunset,
Shining on the calming beach.

Diamond,
A rippling crystal-clear stream,
Gently flowing by.

Opal,
Shining so bright like the
Sparkling stars in a pitch-dark sky.

Ruby,
The colour of red roses lost
In a field of silence.

Natalie Ryan (10)
Llanfaes Community Primary School, Brecon

TEN THINGS FOUND IN A WIZARD'S POCKET

A little stone, red, yellow, green and blue,
A little pointy wand,
A big dragon,
An old spell book,
Some green grass,
A black cauldron,
Some brown and green trees,
A brown owl,
Some red false teeth,
A big broomstick.

Jade Gordan (8)
Llanfaes Community Primary School, Brecon

BONFIRE NIGHT

The fireworks hit a gleamy sky,
Flames fall like autumn leaves,
Then another
And another
Catherine wheels spin,
A dazzling fair in the sky,
Babies cry and scream,
Excited children run,
Suddenly!
People start fading away,
The fire dies down
And the once stormy night,
It's now silent.

Samantha Jones (10)
Llanfaes Community Primary School, Brecon

TEN THINGS FOUND IN A WIZARD'S POCKET

A slimy slug dancing and singing,
Some earrings shining in the dark,
A frog leaping in the sparkling sun,
A magic feather floating in the air,
Some dragon's teeth,
A red and yellow rose,
A chicken clucking,
A magic wand sitting down,
An owl resting quietly,
Some smelly bones.

Laura Harris (7)
Llanfaes Community Primary School, Brecon

BONFIRE NIGHT

Crackle,
Hot dogs and onions flaming hot,
People,
Screaming rockets in the midnight sky,
Fireworks,
Roman candles, screechers, Catherine wheels,
Flames,
Dancing in a coal-black ocean sky,
Colours,
Raging red, lashing lilac, brilliant blue,
The bonfire,
A fire-breathing dragon,
Catherine wheels,
Hypnotise you!
Guy Fawkes thrown on the hungry fire,
Watch him scream for mercy,
As he starts to fade away
The bonfire turns from blazing heat
To a gentle warmth,
People start to fade away
As the fire goes out,
Silence!

Lisa Williams (10)
Llanfaes Community Primary School, Brecon

PRECIOUS STONES

Rare red rubies shimmer in the golden sun,
Diamonds like a mist of clear silk,
Sapphires like an ocean wave in a night storm,
Opal beautiful like a snowdrop dancing as it falls gently to the ground,
Amber is a golden sun in a hot lonely desert.

Hannah Jarman (9)
Llanfaes Community Primary School, Brecon

PRECIOUS STONES

Down in the pitch-black caves,
Crystals glittering, glimmering,
Glowing brightly underground,
Rubies shimmering, gleaming, beaming,
Rich rainbows form in misty skies,
Moonstones brightly polished,
Clear and precious,
Burning bloodstones like the fire and flames
Of bright bonfires,
Roaring like fire-breathing dragons,
Turquoise, a clear liquid wave,
In a sea of silence.

Ellen Thomas (9)
Llanfaes Community Primary School, Brecon

TEN THINGS FOUND IN A WIZARD'S POCKET

Some growing beans which are growing,
A wand which is going cheh chch,
A green baby in a black hat,
Some ghosts that are going, 'Ooooo,'
Some birds going, 'Tweet, tweet,'
Some trolls stamping around,
A huge wolf that is howling really loud,
Some flying clothes,
A flying pen that is writing on paper,
Some false teeth that are biting the
Wizard on the leg.

James Harrison (8)
Llanfaes Community Primary School, Brecon

TEN THINGS FOUND IN A WIZARD'S POCKET

A big shiny mirror,
Some magic rabbits sleeping,
A little book of spells,
Some owls hooting,
A frog jumping up and down,
Some smelly frogs,
A long wand sparkling,
Some big hats poking,
A spider blown to bits,
Some spiders crawling.

Aaron Horne (8)
Llanfaes Community Primary School, Brecon

TEN THINGS FOUND IN A WIZARD'S POCKET

Some old dusty books,
A magical stone with secret powers,
Some gold watches that chime at midnight,
A pen that turns into a wand,
A magic feather,
Some owls,
A spooky spider,
Some cats,
A slimy frog,
A broomstick that flies in the air.

Josh Middleton (8)
Llanfaes Community Primary School, Brecon

PRECIOUS STONES

Red ruby,
Like sparkling blood,
Bloodstone,
Rainbow reflections glowing,
Precious light,
Clear diamonds,
Sunlight mirrors,
Purple amethyst,
Polished precious sparks,
Pearls,
Black, bright beaming raindrops.

Chelsea Raby (9)
Llanfaes Community Primary School, Brecon

FEAR IN THE AIR

I can taste fear in the air,
The dread in the people around me,
The bodies rigid and lifeless as I wait for the Zulus to attack,
I can taste fear in the air,
The smoke choking and burning me,
The blood coming out of the murdered men,
The sweat on my skin salty and chilling
As I wait for the Zulus to attack,
As the silence closes in.
It's over.

Rhys Wyn Williams (10)
Llanfaes Community Primary School, Brecon

I WOULD LIKE TO . . .

I would like to taste some magic beans,
Or smell the flowers on the breeze,

I would like to hear the leopards roar,
Or see a fairy in the sky,

If I could I would eat my mum's big pie,
Or try and touch the birds up high.

Shannon Gallogly (8)
Llanfaes Community Primary School, Brecon

PRECIOUS STONES

Blood stones run through you,
Diamond mirrors in the soft sun,
Ruby-red roses,
Sapphires as blue as the ocean.

Christopher Morris (9)
Llanfaes Community Primary School, Brecon

I WOULD LIKE TO . . .

I would like to jump over a rainbow,
Or shake hands with Winnie the Pooh,
I would like to walk on clouds,
Or meet Mickey Mouse in Paris.

Molly Louise Sweeney (8)
Llanfaes Community Primary School, Brecon

IF DREAMS CAME TRUE

I would like to touch a faraway planet,
Or fly through space to Mars.
I would like to see a heavenly angel,
Or float through the fluffy clouds.
I would like to hear the tigers roar,
Or trek right through the jungle,
I would like to smell the fresh wild flowers,
Or walk through a beautiful meadow.

Emma Haworth (7)
Llanfaes Community Primary School, Brecon

FLYING

I would like to be a bird,
Or a bee in a hive.
I would like to see a jet,
Or be a pilot flying by.

Matthew Hyatt (8)
Llanfaes Community Primary School, Brecon

SHIPS

Sailing ships going through the sea,
Ahoy me mates,
I see land me hearties,
Pirates ahead,
Ship men attack.

Ryan Hopkins (8)
Llanfaes Community Primary School, Brecon

THE SOUND OF BATTLE

Dead bodies screaming with anger,
Shrieking with fear,
Spine-chilling shrieks from Zulu's with fear,
Calling out with deafening anxiousness.

Gunfire crashing,
Booming as loud as can be,
Ears splitting with horror,
Crash, boom, crash, boom!

Blaring commands,
With accurate frequency,
With resounding vibes,
So deafening they make you shiver.

The threatening chanting,
Which pierces your ears,
Thunderous screams,
Deafening roars.

The horn echoing,
Penetrating with fear,
Battle begins,
Boom! Boom!

The battle closes,
Dying bodies shrieking,
Blood bubbling,
Finally battle draws to an end!

Kristy Evans (11)
Llanfaes Community Primary School, Brecon

BONFIRE NIGHT

People whirling down the road,
Children skipping and running,
Parents walking with the dog,
Wishing
They would have just stayed at home,
All the children
Say, 'Wey hey!'
And parents just say, 'Here it is again,
Bonfire Night!'
Booming bombs in the sky,
Like red blood spitting out,
Purple flowers, mixed with blue and gold,
Splashing through the midnight sky,
Dogs barking,
Growling too,
Cats miaow,
Screaming babies,
Crackling fireworks as they depart,
Swinging like leaves as they drop like raindrops,
After, children cry
As the fireworks fade.
The end is here,
As children and parents slow
Down as they walk home.

Hannah Rowe (10)
Llanfaes Community Primary School, Brecon

TEN THINGS FOUND IN A WIZARD'S POCKET

A magical wand with dust on the top of it,
A scary spider creeping up the wall.

Some shiny money that is being paid,
Some magical dust floating in the air.

Some dusty feathers waiting to be cleaned,
A vase that is nice and big.

A slimy frog swimming in the pond,
Some teeth that are rotten.

An old dusty book that makes me sneeze,
Some old gel pens that don't work anymore.

Sophie Watkins (7)
Llanfaes Community Primary School, Brecon

TEN THINGS IN A WIZARD'S POCKET

A big fluffy rabbit eating a juicy carrot,
Some big fat toads jumping around like rabbits,
A long glass wand casting spells on princes,
A big shiny mirror reflecting in the sun,
Some bats waiting to be eaten,
An old rusty pen,
Some magic wizard's dust,
A petal of a magic tulip,
Some white farm wool,
A red sweet whistle.

Angharad Stephens (7)
Llanfaes Community Primary School, Brecon

THE SOUND OF THE BATTLE!

The sound of loud courageous singing as the soldiers wait,
The roaring chanting as the Zulus approach,
The rigid commands that are yelled.

The danger of death that's furious,
The fear that's scary beating against horror,
The anger that hurts.

The Zulus charging, running and rushing,
The explosions - *bang! Crash!*
The scream of death, I'm frightened,
The gunfire charged at me speedily,
Bang! Bang!

Sarah Johnston (10)
Llanfaes Community Primary School, Brecon

TEN THINGS FOUND IN A WIZARD'S POCKET

A barking dog with black spots,
Some magic dust glittering,
A sparkling cauldron,
Some dusty spell books,
A naughty broomstick,
Some fire candles,
A funky rabbit looking at you,
Some slimy frogs,
A scary dog,
A dusty wand.

Dale Williams (8)
Llanfaes Community Primary School, Brecon

SENSES

I would like to taste some fizzy sweets,
I would like to hear the drummer's beat,
I would like to smell the heat of my tea,
I would like to see the bumblebees,
I would like to touch the man in the moon,
Who lives alone in space.

Luli Boyd (8)
Llanfaes Community Primary School, Brecon

MILLION

I would like to see a million stars,
Or touch the yellow sun,
I would like to smell the sweetest petal,
Or taste the juiciest fruit.
I would like to be the man in the moon,
Or win a million pounds.

Davey Herdman (8)
Llanfaes Community Primary School, Brecon

THINGS I LIKE DOING

I would like to taste a wriggly worm,
Or see the PM in Downing Street.
I would like to smell the scent of the meadows,
Or hear the sound of God's voice.
I would like to touch an angel in Heaven.

Jack Jones (9)
Llanfaes Community Primary School, Brecon

I LIVE - I FEAR

I feel the bitter blood run through me,
The pain and fear is bewitching,
I live - I fear!
The pain encircles me from every direction,
Is it power or defeat I feel?
Death is around the corner,
Waiting, waiting.

Emma Davies (11)
Llanfaes Community Primary School, Brecon

I WOULD LIKE TO . . .

I would like to taste snails in Sweden,
Or touch a million pounds.

I would like to smell the fresh fluffy clouds,
Or see the man on the moon.

Jake Newman (8)
Llanfaes Community Primary School, Brecon

STARS

S   hooting stars racing through space,
T   winkling like bright night lights,
A   bove the world they shine so high,
R   iding around the Earth,
S   hining down on us.

Naomi Haworth (8)
Llanfaes Community Primary School, Brecon

MAGIC WONDERS

I would like to taste ice cream in India,
Or touch a million stars,
I would like to smell the most perfumed flower,
Or see a thousand rainbows.
I would like to hear the tiger roar,
Or touch a coral reef.

Beatrice Wigmore (7)
Llanfaes Community Primary School, Brecon

I WOULD LIKE . . .

I would like to smell a bunch of bluebells
Or taste the biggest chocolate bar,
I would like to touch 2,000 or see a shoal of dolphins,
I would like to hear waves crashing on the rocks.

Louise Payne (8)
Llanfaes Community Primary School, Brecon

UP IN THE SKY

I would like to taste some fluffy clouds,
Or touch the moon every day,
I would like to smell the burning stars
Or see the planet Mars.

Kate Williams (8)
Llanfaes Community Primary School, Brecon

A DAY IN SPACE

I would like to touch a million puffy clouds,
Or taste the Milky Way,
I would like to see planet Mercury,
Or smell the atmosphere,
I would like to hear the twinkling stars and
Slide down the sun
Oh that would be fun!

Alice Wolstenholme (8)
Llanfaes Community Primary School, Brecon

MAN UNITED

I would like to taste Van Nistelrooy's drink,
Or touch Man United's pitch.

I would like to smell Beckham's sweaty shirt,
Or see them win the cup.

Josh Davies (8)
Llanfaes Community Primary School, Brecon

LIONS

L   eopards running away,
I   n the distance, a flamingo struts by,
O   strich flapping their wings in play,
N   ewts basking in the sun,
S   quirrels running up the tree having fun.

Rhys Evans (9)
Llanfaes Community Primary School, Brecon

PLANETS

I would like to hear the rockets blow,
I would like to taste alien food,
I would like to touch the hot planet Mars,
I would like to see a UFO hovering,
I would like to smell the gases spitting out of the sun.

Scott Bowen (8)
Llanfaes Community Primary School, Brecon

SENSES

I would like to taste frogs' legs in France,
Or touch a million pounds,
I would like to smell unleaded petrol,
Or see new life from a baby,
I would like to hear a snake's tail rattle
And if I could . . . I would!

Luke Roughley (8)
Llanfaes Community Primary School, Brecon

WHAT I LIKE . . .

I would like to taste the snails in France,
I would like to smell petrol from the ground,
I would like to touch the planet Mars,
I would like to see a shooting star
I would like to hear a rocket roar,
I would like to do all these things.

Ceiran Jones (9)
Llanfaes Community Primary School, Brecon

MY TWO FAVOURITE PUPPIES

The time has come and the puppies have to go
Although I must not let my sadness show.
Each time I see a sheepdog puppy I will think of them
and it will make me happy.
Each day they had was a happy day, although
each day they had was a different day.
I myself don't know what to say
but I will miss them every time I play.
Happy memories remain for some:
The way they tucked themselves up in their cosy bed.
The way they waited to be fed.
Their coat, as smooth as golden silk,
Their faces as white as morning milk.
In the morning they chased the sparrows.
The thought of them going hits you like a poisoned arrow.
The time has come to say goodbye,
Tears fill my eyes and I start to cry.

Colleen Baker (10)
Llanfihangel Rhydithon CP School, Llandrindod Wells

RICE PUDDING

Mushed with chocolate,
A muddy, sticky pond.
Tiny fish dash to the surface.
An enormous monstrous net dips into the pond.
Nobody survives.
'It's only rice pudding,' says my sister,
Licking her spoon.

Leanne Jones (10)
Llanfihangel Rhydithon CP School, Llandrindod Wells

MERINGUES

Today we're going to my nan's.
I know what we're having for a snack.
Meringue.
A sheet of hard, crispy, pointy,
Meringue.
Slices of pears and apples
As glistening treetops.
Meringue.
Pineapple as children trying so hard,
Pulling their sledges up the hill.
Meringue.
Bananas like boulders of snow,
Hanging by a thread.
Meringue.
Yellow, lumpy, white custard,
As a shimmering, delicate iced-over river,
Travelling down an avalanched hill.
Meringue.
I dig my spoon under the meringue.
It's like a dark cave,
With stalactites and stalagmites.
Meringue.
My nan comes in and better still,
She's coming in with ice cream.
Yum! Yum! Ice cream.
I suppose the meringue wasn't too bad.
Meringue.

Jessica Kennedy (10)
Llanfihangel Rhydithon CP School, Llandrindod Wells

THE BUSY JUNGLE TOWN

Treetop shops with busy buyers,
Fighting and shoving to get the best things.
The big fat elephant brings lots of anxious shoppers.
Beautiful and dazzling the bright birds sit.

'Step right up,' the ant sellers squeak.
The cheetah runs all over the town,
Crawling and running on the little monkeys' feet,
As they buy all the leaves for the winter.

Joshua Birch (11)
Llanfihangel Rhydithon CP School, Llandrindod Wells

CHICKEN CURRY AND CHIPS

I shape my rice into a volcanic dip.
Then I pour the hot, spicy curry into the hollow.
The curry bubbles over like lava.
Chips are like trees that plunge down the slope.
The look of it makes my tummy erupt.
It steams like a volcano as it enters my mouth.

Kevin Davies (10)
Llanfihangel Rhydithon CP School, Llandrindod Wells

THE POND (AS A WASHING-UP BOWL)

Translucent plates like delicate lily pads.
Empty cups, hard as caves.
Fishy knives swimming.
Foam, soft and bubbly.

Rosa Kennard (9)
Llanfihangel Rhydithon CP School, Llandrindod Wells

SPAGHETTI BOLOGNESE

Scooping up my Bolognese,
Don't know what I'll find.
Swampy, gooey snakes crawling,
Up your fork like spaghetti strings.
Cheese gliding through the dirty water,
Like swift crocodiles.
When I stick in my fork,
Slurping and gooey in my mouth.
Bolognese like swampy water,
Around my face.

Darrilyn Ruell (11)
Llanfihangel Rhydithon CP School, Llandrindod Wells

THE MARMITE OIL SPILLAGE

Dipping through the foil,
On our Marmite jar,
Yippee! I have just struck oil.
The rich, dark, gloopy paste will not drop off
As much as I shake.
Oh no! Mum's gone crazy.
I have a drop of Marmite
On my new trousers.
I smeared my hands all down them.
The deadly smell lives on my hands.

Rebekah Bufton (10)
Llanfihangel Rhydithon CP School, Llandrindod Wells

HIDDEN TREASURES

These marbles I found,
In a cave by the sea,
Under the ground,
Special to me.

This shawl which I've had,
Since we lived in the south,
And I fell asleep,
With it still in my mouth.

A tea set which stays,
At the top of my shelf,
I've know it as long as
I've known myself.

And these treasures I keep,
That no one can see,
Just memories of past times,
So precious to me.

Brodie Hayward (10)
Llangynidr CP School, Crickhowell

HIDDEN TREASURES

The key that I love, is but one in the land,
I love to hold it really tight in my hand.
I've tried and I've tried to find the special door,
But sometimes I think, could it be something more?

Could this one key open a million doors?
Could this key prevent a million wars?
This key that I found on the shore in the sand,
My love for this key will forever expand.

Sarah Cartwright (11)
Llangynidr CP School, Crickhowell

MY HIDDEN TREASURES

These rabbits I keep at the bottom of the garden,
Brown eyes, fur jet-black and grey,
Nobody can fuss them or touch them,
At the bottom of the garden lying in the hay.

I got them long ago,
One for 50p,
Nobody thought they were special,
Except me.

These rabbits I keep at the bottom of the garden,
Brown eyes, fur jet-black and grey,
Nobody can fuss them or touch them,
At the bottom of the garden lying in the hay.

I got my first rabbit at the sales,
In a small cardboard box,
I lock him away at the end of the day,
So he doesn't get eaten by the fox.

These rabbits I keep at the bottom of the garden,
Brown eyes, fur jet-black and grey,
Nobody can fuss them or touch them,
At the bottom of the garden lying in the hay.

My second rabbit, I bred her myself,
She is very cute and fluffy,
With a small spot on her nose,
I keep her in a pen next to my old goat, Muffy.

These rabbits I keep at the bottom of the garden,
Brown eyes, fur jet-black and grey,
Nobody can fuss them or touch them,
At the bottom of the garden lying in the hay.

They are mine and no one else's,
So don't try to see,
If I do ever catch you,
You'll answer to me!

These rabbits I keep at the bottom of the garden,
Brown eyes, fur jet-black and grey,
Nobody can fuss them or touch them,
At the bottom of the garden lying in the hay.

Rosie Whiting (11)
Llangynidr CP School, Crickhowell

HIDDEN TREASURES

My treasures are hidden where nobody knows
In the back of the cupboard among the old clothes,
The first is an eagle's egg stone,
My granny gave it to me before I went home,
It is round and smooth and yellow and red,
And I put it in a box in a tissue bed.

The next is my blue diamond stone,
I can't remember
Who gave it me, though,
It's a very odd shape, a sort of square,
I put it in a box and hid it somewhere,
But now I come to think of it, I don't know where!

My final treasure isn't really mine,
It's a black china dog with the eyes of a lime,
It's my mum's special treasure
And I look at it with pleasure,
At the back of the wardrobe where nobody goes,
In a box amongst toys and very old clothes.

Elizabeth Pollard (10)
Llangynidr CP School, Crickhowell

MY LITTLE WHITE PEBBLE

My little white pebble,
Lies down in its box,
Where no one will know,
It came from the docks.

My grandad gave it to me,
When I went to see
If he was OK,
That dull windy day.

No one can touch it,
It's my special thing,
It lies in its box,
And it lives with my socks.

My little white pebble,
Lies down in its box,
Where no one will know,
It came from the docks.

Faye Perry (10)
Llangynidr CP School, Crickhowell

TRUTHFULNESS

Truthfulness is the white of clouds,
It tastes of yellow lemons,
It looks like air in the sky.
Truthfulness is the sound of family fun,
A game with my friends and family,
Truthfulness makes me happy.

Natasha Euston (8)
Llwynypia Primary School, Tonypandy

ROBIN BEGAN

She took the softness from the clouds
She took the hopping from a child jumping
She took the white from delicate snow
She took the eyes from deep wells.

She took the tail from a puffed-up ball
She took the nose from a gentle wild flower
She took the feet from a long, wide stick to fit her feet
She took the ears from flip-flops.

She took the nails from sharp spears
She took the teeth from the sharpness of dripping icicles
She took the small back feet from wide pebbles
She took the bones from dry sticks.

And *Rabbit* was made.

Rachel Clapp (11)
Llwynypia Primary School, Tonypandy

DOLPHIN BEGAN

She took silk for her smooth skin.

She took a smile for her friendly face.

She took a soft walk for her smooth glide.

She took soft snow for her white belly.

She took darkness from the sky for her eyes.

She took a whip of lightning for her tail.

And *Dolphin* began.

Hayley Thomas (10)
Llwynypia Primary School, Tonypandy

DOLPHIN BEGAN

She stole her glistening eyes from the pearls
of a seven-string necklace.

She formed her long mouth from an
extremely tall javelin.

She took her silky skin from the inside of the
dark damp caves.

She grabbed her sleek and slender shape
from the Milky Way.

She took her sky-blue fins from the
silent night moon.

She took her wet tail from the slender
curve of the morn.

And *Dolphin* was born.

Leah Thomas (10)
Llwynypia Primary School, Tonypandy

SPIDER BEGAN

Spider took his devastating venom,
from the deadly blood of a predator.

Spider's silk web is spun from the spring-
water gushing through the air.

His tiny eyes survey his prey as a
destroyer waits for the final kill.

And *Spider* was born!

Andrew Bayliss (10)
Llwynypia Primary School, Tonypandy

TIGER BEGAN

He took the swaying of the trees
And the breeze of the wind
To make his walk.

He took the sharpness of ice
And the whiteness of an icicle
To make his teeth.

He took the glinting of a diamond
And the roundness of the sun
To make his eyes.

He took the sharpness of a knife
And the length of an infinite galaxy
To produce his claws.

He took the roar of a bear
And the screeching of an owl
To make his voice

And *Tiger* was made.

Daniel Tucker (11)
Llwynypia Primary School, Tonypandy

HAPPINESS

Happiness is the yellow of the sun,
It tastes of lemons,
It looks like sundrops.
Love is the sound of birds singing,
A disco with my friends,
Love makes me happy.

David Lee (9)
Llwynypia Primary School, Tonypandy

TIGER BEGAN

For his eyes
He took his glaring eyes from an owl's stare
He took his furtive glare from a still scarecrow

For his fangs
He took his fangs from razor-sharp blades
He took deadly icicles for his fangs

For his voice
He took his fierce roar from the gushing wind
He took his hungry snarl from a vicious grizzly bear

For his movement
He took the moving of the rapid water for stealthy speed
He took the deadly silence of the eerie depths of the ocean

For his coat
He took his black striped fur from gloomy caves in Antarctica
He took his orange stripes from a Venus sunset.

And *Tiger* was made.

Leon Williams (10)
Llwynypia Primary School, Tonypandy

HAPPINESS

Happiness is the red of Man U,
It tastes of lemons,
It looks like a Man U top.
Happiness is the sound of birds singing,
A football game with my friends,
It makes me really happy.

Jordan Erricker (8)
Llwynypia Primary School, Tonypandy

TIGER BEGAN

Tiger began

He took the haunted howl of the whirling wind
He took the vicious snarl of a hungry bear
And made his voice.

He took the bright yellow stripes of the golden sand
He took the black stripes of a thousand mines
And made his coat.

He took his gripping furtive stance from the ocean's current
He took his slender moves from a slithering snake
And made his walk.

He took the golden brightness of the glowing moon
He took the bright glow of the glistening stars
And made his eyes.

He took the superior sharpness of a deadly spear
He took the slender curve of a half moon
And made his claws.

And *Tiger* was made.

Molly Vincent (10)
Llwynypia Primary School, Tonypandy

HAPPINESS

Happiness is the blue of the shiny sky,
It tastes of juicy apples,
It looks like a happy family,
Happiness is the sound of birds singing,
A party with lots of friends,
Happiness makes me kind.

Joshua Lewis (8)
Llwynypia Primary School, Tonypandy

SNAKE BEGAN

For its hiss
It took the slither of silk
It took the whisper of a spiteful mood
It took the sharp kiss of respite.

For its eyes
It took two glints of the moon
It took the depths of the universe
It took the twin eyes of a pin.

For its length
It took the crack of a whip
It took the swiftness of a lasso
It got the curl of a slender tongue.

For its form
It took the stealth of a cat at night
It took the sway of the ocean's current
It took the shadows of the branches of the trees.

And *Snake* was made.

Emma-Jayne Morgan (10)
Llwynypia Primary School, Tonypandy

HAPPINESS

Happiness is the pink of a cake,
It tastes of pink icing,
It looks like a loving family.
Happiness is the sound of birds singing,
A party with friends,
Happiness makes me joyful.

Katie Hadley (8)
Llwynypia Primary School, Tonypandy

FEAR

Fear is the red of blood,
It tastes like juicy eyeballs,
It looks like dead bodies.
Fear is the sound of screaming,
A killing game.
Fear makes me *s h i v e r!*

Ethan Davies (9)
Llwynypia Primary School, Tonypandy

HAPPINESS

Happiness is the red of lips,
It tastes of strawberry cake,
It looks like families playing,
Music is the sound of love,
A girl and boy with feelings.
Singing makes me happy.

Carrie Jane Studley (8)
Llwynypia Primary School, Tonypandy

HAPPINESS

Happiness is the red of roses,
It tastes of lemon cake,
It looks like a small family.
Happiness is the sound of birds singing,
A party with friends,
Happiness makes me happy.

Matthew Dendle (8)
Llwynypia Primary School, Tonypandy

TIGER BEGAN

He took his superior strength
From the hardness of a tree.

He took his sleek and slender form
From the heart of the ocean's swirling depth.

He took his white vicious teeth
From the sharpness of a thousand swords.

He took his deadly vicious claws
From the curve of the moon.

He took his piercing eyes
From the sharpness of sharks' teeth.

And Tiger was made.

Rhys Gillard (10)
Llwynypia Primary School, Tonypandy

DOLPHIN BEGAN

Dolphin began

She took her shiny silky skin from
The walls of the damp dark caves.

She took her blue crystal eyes from
A seven-string pearl necklace.

She took her snowy under-belly from
The whiteness and softness of the clouds.

She took her long smooth mouth from
A tall jumping javelin thrower.

And *Dolphin* was made.

Carly Crichton (11)
Llwynypia Primary School, Tonypandy

LION BEGAN

Lion began.
He took the moving of the whipping water
He took the silence of stones to make his sleek walk.

He took the roaring of the fierce wind
He took the loudness of thunder to make his terrifying voice.

He took the colours of sunset
He took the softness of velvet and silk to make his fur.

He took the sharpness of a knife
He took the whiteness of the moon to make his razor-sharp teeth.

He took the glittering of the stars
He took the brownness of autumn leaves to make his piercing eyes.

And *Lion* was made.

Rebecca Hull (10)
Llwynypia Primary School, Tonypandy

TIGER BEGAN

He took the colour of the sun to make his golden coat.

He took the movement of the ocean's silent current to make his walk.

He took the sharpness of a spear to make his teeth.

He took the feather of a blackbird to make his stripes.

He took a whip to make his tail.

He took the claws from daggers to tear his prey open.

He took the glittering out of the stars to make his eyes.

He took mice tails to make his whiskers.

Nathan Hughes (10)
Llwynypia Primary School, Tonypandy

HATE

Hate is the red of blood,
It tastes of red roses,
It looks like a madhouse.
Hate is the sound of screaming,
A room on your own in the dark,
Hate makes me mad.

Rebekah Sparrow (8)
Llwynypia Primary School, Tonypandy

FEAR

Fear is the red of blood,
It tastes of squashed eyeballs,
It looks like a human body.
Fear is the sound of screaming,
A creepy skeleton.
Fear makes me scream.

Jed Burnell (8)
Llwynypia Primary School, Tonypandy

HAPPINESS

Happiness is the red of a rose,
It tastes of red apples,
It looks like a lovely round ball,
Happiness is the sound of a squirrel munching,
Football with my mates.
Happiness makes me cry.

Grant Davies (9)
Llwynypia Primary School, Tonypandy

EAGLE BEGAN

Eagle began
He stole the length of a python outstretched,
And stole the downy feathers of a thousand extinct dodos,
And his wings were created.

He stole the sharpness of a million razor blades.
He stole the tip of a deadly, murdering mountain,
And stole the new moon's slender curve,
And his beak was created.

He stole the beady glaring eyes of an owl hunting for mice,
And stole the night vision from a sniper rifle,
And stole the darkness of an elderberry,
And his eyes were created.

He stole the sharp spikes from the top of the Himalayas,
And stole the length of a walrus's long, sharp, white, glistening teeth,
And his claws were created.

He stole the loud screech of the howling wind,
And stole the whipping of the branches of the gnarled trees,
And stole the screech of an owl,
And formed his voice.

He stole the glide of a barn owl slowly dropping to the ground,
And stole the skill, superior strength and savage hunting skills
                                                            of a hawk,
And formed his flight.

    And *Eagle* was born.

Adam Port (9)
Llwynypia Primary School, Tonypandy

HAPPINESS

Happiness is the yellow of the sundrops,
It tastes of sweethearts,
It looks like a rainbow in the sky.
Happiness is the sound of raindrops,
A feast with my friends,
Happiness makes me joyful.

Sarah Bayliss (8)
Llwynypia Primary School, Tonypandy

FEAR

Fear is the black of a dungeon,
It tastes of lemons so bitter,
It looks like a knife in the heart.
Fear is the sound of a roaring monster.
A dead body in your house.
Fear makes me shiver.

Joshua Vaughan (8)
Llwynypia Primary School, Tonypandy

HAPPINESS

Happiness is the blue of the sky,
It tastes of bubblegum,
It looks like a caring family,
Happiness is the sound of birds singing,
A party with friends to play with.
Happiness makes me kind.

Nathan Farr (9)
Llwynypia Primary School, Tonypandy

LION BEGAN

He created his mighty roar from
The thunder of the darkest of loud, howling skies.

He created his large crystal teeth from
The sharp tips of the sharpest man-killing spears.

He created his soft, illuminating cashmere coat from
The burning bright sun of the sky.

He created his huge padded paws from
The silent stealth of a murderous wolf.

He created his cold dark eyes from
The sleek furtive Devil from deep, red *Hell.*

He created his sleek, slender form from
The sunset, summer's horizon.

He created his superior strength from
The big brown bear from the forests.

He created his masterful muscles from
The great grey rhino of Africa.

He created his silent, rapid pounce from
The largest, quickest hares.

And *Lion* was made.

Nicholas Adams (11)
Llwynypia Primary School, Tonypandy

HAPPINESS

Happiness is the orange of sunshine,
It tastes of jelly,
It looks like bungee-jumping
Happiness is the sound of birds singing,
A football game with my friends,
Happiness makes me laugh.

Joshua Embling (8)
Llwynypia Primary School, Tonypandy

HAPPINESS

Happiness is the red of strawberry,
It tastes of birthday cake,
It looks like a happy family.
Happiness is the sound of birds singing,
A dancing competition with children
Happiness makes me happy.

Elysia Dione Williams (8)
Llwynypia Primary School, Tonypandy

HAPPINESS

Happiness is the yellow of sun,
It tastes like watermelon,
It looks like a joyful family playing
It's the sound of birds singing,
A party with lots of friends
It makes me feel happy.

Leah Hughes (8)
Llwynypia Primary School, Tonypandy

FEAR

Fear is the red of blood,
It tastes of juicy eyeballs,
It looks like a dead body,
Fear is the sound of screaming,
A killing monster game,
Fear makes me die.

Jay Bradley (8)
Llwynypia Primary School, Tonypandy

HAPPINESS

Happiness is the blue of the sky,
It tastes of football cake,
It looks like a loving family.
Happiness is the sound like laughter,
A game of basketball with my friends,
Happiness makes me happy.

Elliott Hayward (9)
Llwynypia Primary School, Tonypandy

HATE

Hate is the blackness of a dungeon,
It tastes sour,
It looks like a monster.
Hate is the sound of banging,
A disco with no friends,
Hate makes me scared.

Samantha Burman (8)
Llwynypia Primary School, Tonypandy

WOLF BEGAN

He took his fur from a deadly polar bear, lush and soft
like smooth snow on a fearsome mountain.

He took his eyes from a deep dark cave
where you can see his eyes light up in the dark.

He took his sharp teeth from a killer shark,
dangerous to all other animals.

He took his fearsome paws like a sword moving
in the air, killing all as he hunted.

He took his tail from the moving of the wind,
whistling through forests and mountains.

And *Wolf* was born.

Jarrad Davies (10)
Llwynypia Primary School, Tonypandy

LION BEGAN

Lion began.

He took his glaring eyes from vicious fire.
For his fur he took the gold of glittering stars.

He took the mournful howl of the piercing
wind and made his voice.

For his claws he took the sharpness of the razor.

He took the movement of water for his walk.

For his teeth he took Antarctica's pointed ice.

And *Lion* was made.

Kayleigh Butt (11)
Llwynypia Primary School, Tonypandy

SHARK BEGAN

He took his dazzling white teeth
from the vampire's bloodthirsty fangs.

He took his tiny, beady eyes
from the glint of a star.

He took his superior, unbelievable strength
from a healthy tiger.

He took his vicious strange fins
from a sharp javelin.

He took his leathery wet skin
from the heart of the ocean's depths.

And Shark was made.

Cyle Jenkins (10)
Llwynypia Primary School, Tonypandy

BUNNY BEGAN

She took her white fur coat
From a polar bear grizzling in the Antarctic.

She took her large white whiskers
From a sharp icicle coming from the ground.

She took her white fluffy bobtail
From the softness of a rug.

She took the whiteness of her ears
From the glittering of the stars.

She took the brightness of her eyes
From the glowing of the full moon.

Aimee Harries (11)
Llwynypia Primary School, Tonypandy

HORSE BEGAN

For his ears
he took the shape
from the slender
curve of the moon.

For his nose
he took the hole
from a dark
recess of a cave.

For his legs
he took the length of
a galloping river.

For his eyes
he took the glistening of
the shining stars.

For his tail
he took the light brown
fragrant straw.

For his coat
he took the blackness
of a dark sky.

Leah-Marie Newman (10)
Llwynypia Primary School, Tonypandy

TIGER BEGAN

He took black stripes from the strike of lightning.
He took his sharp claws from the teeth of a shark.
He took his superior strength from a grey rock.

He took his terror from a black damp cave.
He took his loud roar from the howling wind.
He took his orange skin from a burning flame.

He took his movement from the flow of the tide.
He took the roughness of his tongue from sandpaper.
He took his big paws from an enormous rock.

He took his sharp teeth from the end of an icicle.
He took his eyes from pearls of the ocean.
He took his raging roar from the gushing wind.

And *Tiger* was made.

Emily Evans (10)
Llwynypia Primary School, Tonypandy

HARVEST

Walking to school in the autumn
Under the bare, stripped trees
Trudging down the pavement
Through the crunchy, crisp leaves.

Walking to school in the autumn
Frost and dew on the grass
Running down the road
To get to class.

Walking to school in the autumn
Through the nippy air
Running through the car park
Coldness everywhere.

I'm at school in the autumn
And now it's harvest time
It's worth going to school right now
When it's Thanksgiving time.

Arianne Hopkins (10)
Mount Street Junior School, Brecon

THOMAS WOLSEY

Thomas Wolsey is the colour of smooth scarlet
In the hot, sunny summer at Hampton Court Palace.
He is a long pearl chain with a golden cross
Ruling over the King's Council in York.
He is a lovely, deep-sounding cello
A beautiful white, glistening Siberian tiger
And he is the sound of the trumpet calling his arrival.

Kimberley Tinegate (10)
Mount Street Junior School, Brecon

PEACE

Peace is the colour of blue and cream,
Peace smells like love and fresh air,
Peace tastes like a tasteful ice cream,
Peace sounds of joyful birds singing in the sky,
Peace feels like a relaxing room,
And peace lives in Heaven.

Lauren Griffin (10)
Mount Street Junior School, Brecon

HOPE

Hope is white,
And smells of sweet honey,
Hope tastes of smooth sweets,
It sounds like birds,
Hope is smooth and soft,
And lives in good and Heaven.

James Cave (9)
Mount Street Junior School, Brecon

WAR

War is the colour of darkest black,
War smells like thick smoke,
War tastes like blood and pain,
War sounds like guns and bombs,
War feels like pain and death,
War lives in Hell!

Tomos Prosser (10)
Mount Street Junior School, Brecon

PEACE

Peace is the colour of creamy white
Peace smells like a daisy blowing in the wind
Peace tastes like nice pleasant food
Peace sounds like birds singing in the trees
Peace feels like a white blanket
Peace lives in a bird's heart.

Luc Greaves (9)
Mount Street Junior School, Brecon

FRIENDSHIP

Friendship is the colour of red and pink.
It smells like red roses in a bunch.
It tastes like friendship, eating yoghurt.
It feels like friendship, people hugging.
It sounds like friendship, birds singing.
It lives in a place where no one knows.

Shai Cutts (9)
Mount Street Junior School, Brecon

WAR FEELINGS

War is deadly,
Bringing pain to an injured soldier,
Anxiety for his family at home,
Fighting, fighting, fighting.

War is loneliness,
Bringing misery to a worried mother,
Terrified for her child,
Hoping, hoping, hoping.

War is frightening,
Bringing confusion to an evacuee,
Wishing for his parents,
Weeping, weeping, weeping.

Antony Jenkins (10)
Mount Street Junior School, Brecon

WAR IS HORRIBLE

War is like a dark graveyard.
The people rise from the ground.
His heart beats like a hammer.
He might get killed and then he will be put in a grave.

War is like his mother beating him up.
It makes him feel terrified.
He wants to cry.
He doesn't cry because he swallows his tears.

War is like a big fat cat fighting a little kitten.
Claws expand and fur stands on end.
He just wants to go back in front of the fire.
The cosy home where his owner loves him.

Harry Casaru (11)
Mount Street Junior School, Brecon

WORLD WAR II

War is fear
Trying to be brave
But fear is growing inside
Going to war with heavy guns
Pictures of your family
In the bag on your back
Trying to keep the sound of crying out
But you can't fight it, war is here.

War is crying
As your children are being taken away
You may never see them again
Worried about your husband at war
Saying to yourself, 'He will live,'
Holding on to your gas mask
Being prepared
But you can't fight it, war is here.

War is nervousness
Being evacuated
Missing your mum very much
Hoping that you will see her again
Thinking about your father at war
People being brave going to war
You could never do it
But you can't fight it, war is here.

Kelly Price (10)
Mount Street Junior School, Brecon

BICYCLES

Riding on a bike is fun,
in the warmth of the midday sun.
Cycling along the canal track,
you can hear the ducks go, 'Quack.'
Canal boats going past,
life on a bike is fast,
every day you can whizz along,
so you can never be glum.

Daniel Thomas (8)
Mount Street Junior School, Brecon

RIDE

If you want to take a ride
on the open tide
come with me
and you will see
we'll row, row, row
until we drop right low
home we'll float
in our little wooden boat.

Martyn Hodgetts (10)
Mount Street Junior School, Brecon

MY INVISIBLE FRIEND

My invisible friend
Plays with me till the day is at its end.
He makes me feel happy
He used to change my nappy.

He used to laugh with me.
He even once bounced me on his knee.
We used to watch the sun go down
Even then we saw a funny clown,
                dancing all around the town.

Carys Jones (9)
Mount Street Junior School, Brecon

MONTHS OF THE YEAR

Every year the same months come
starts with January, then comes February.
Soon comes March, then comes
April next it's May.
Then it's the summer, that's June, July
and not forgetting August.
We want summer to stay but it has to go.
We don't like the cold but we like the snow.

Chloe Hill (7)
Mount Street Junior School, Brecon

FIREWORKS

Climbing up tall and bright,
Then burst into showers of starry light.
Then down and down they will go,
Right down to the ground below.
Then another, up again,
Then falling down into the lane.
Fireworks take to flight,
But only work in the night.

Imogen Hosie (8)
Mount Street Junior School, Brecon

HAPPINESS

Happiness is the colour of red
Happiness is the smell of a mint leaf
Happiness is the taste of a strawberry sweet
Happiness is the sound of a bluebird
Happiness feels like a soft, lime, fluffy mat
Happiness lives in our bright orange room.

Samantha Lewis (9) & Rachel Clowes (10)
Mount Street Junior School, Brecon

THE SEA

The beautiful blue sea,
crashing against rocks.
The angry sea splashing in temper,
Seaweed floating ashore.
A lighthouse standing proudly,
guiding boats safely along.
Now it's become calm and still.

Amanda Baker (11)
Mount Street Junior School, Brecon

AUTUMN

A   is for apples, fresh from the tree
U   is for umbrellas to keep the rain off.
T   is for tomatoes, ripe, rosy and red
U   is for underground stores of squirrels' nuts,
M   is for melon and marrow and mangoes.
N   is for nuts that the squirrels collect.
            I love the colours of autumn.

Bronnie Jones (7)
Mount Street Junior School, Brecon

ODD SOCKS

I can't seem to find a matching sock in our house.
I think we must have a sock-eating mouse.
I've tried buying new socks - pair after pair,
But I can't seem to find them anywhere.
I find dozens of odd socks, ones I didn't know I had,
Some belong to my sister, my mum and my dad,
But none of them make a pair for me.
Why don't you, Sock Mouse, just leave my socks be?

Catrin Sîan Lewis (9)
Mount Street Junior School, Brecon

MY BROTHER

I've got a baby brother
For short we call him Cally
He gets into trouble all the time
He's a little scally
He likes to hit us on the head
But he is a good boy to go to bed.

    I will always love my brother, Callum.

Abby Page (9)
Mount Street Junior School, Brecon

WAR

War is the colour of black.
It lives in a world of pain.
It's murder and death.
It is heartless.
It lives in a rough world.

Lee Brooks (10)
Mount Street Junior School, Brecon

IN THE DEAD OF NIGHT!

In the dead of night
I can hear a shout
It gives me a fright
I cannot get out

    In the dead of night
    Dead bodies come out
    And the way they fight
    Makes me run and shout

In the dead of night
It goes on and on
When I can't see a light
And all my toys have gone

    In the dead of night
    My dolls have run
    My face turns white
    As I wait for the sun.

In the dead of night
With the moon still up
Big and bright
The ghouls don't give up.

    In the dead of night
    I search for the switch
    What's that over there?
    It's OK, my mum's a . . .
                witch!

Jessica Tait (8)
Mount Street Junior School, Brecon

THE YEAR 3000

It is the year three thousand,
And things are different now.
And in this little poem,
I'm going to tell you how.

We don't have electricity,
Or gas or oil for power.
We generate it from the sun,
Through a tall thin tower.

Cities are mainly underground,
With parks and pools on top.
We jump in a space train bubble,
And zap from shop to shop.

They work us very hard at school,
But then our time's our own.
I play with Wis my doll
And Game Boy when I get home.

Computers are in every room,
We hardly move about.
They do every bit of work
As soon as we give the sound.

Samantha Davies (9)
Mount Street Junior School, Brecon

GOING ON HOLIDAY

Going on holiday,
Time to pack,
Trying to fit all my stuff,
Into one big sack!

We are all off to Greece,
To get some peace!
Our hotel is one of the best,
Dad and Moll get lots of rest!

I go to the Thomson Kids' Club,
In the shower I go rub-a-dub-dub,
Then in the evening to the restaurant,
That is what I want!

Then it's time to go!

Holly Watts (10)
Mount Street Junior School, Brecon

HOUSES

Houses come in different shapes and sizes.
Some people even win them for prizes.

A window, a door, a key lock
And more.

Tall ones, small ones, all different shaped ones.
Big ones weigh tonnes.

Bathrooms, bedrooms, front rooms and halls
Carpet, bricks, curtains and walls.

Houses come in different shapes and sizes.

Cara Davies (9)
Mount Street Junior School, Brecon

DESPAIR

Despair is the colour of gone-off dung
It smells of rotten eggs
Despair tastes like acid
It sounds like screaming ghosts
It feels like fire
It lives in Hell!

Benjamin John Rees (9)
Mount Street Junior School, Brecon

YOU'RE A ...

You're a golden delicious pineapple,
waiting to be picked.

You're the colours of the rainbow
shining brightly in the sky.

You're a big base drum,
vibrating.

You're orange juice,
tasty and sweet.

You're my mum,
running the bath.

You're my big, blue sweatshirt,
warm and soft.

You're Big Ben,
in London City.

You're the feeling of my friends,
smiling happily at me.

Alex Wilson (9)
St Mary's Catholic Primary School, Newtown

MY MAGIC BOX

I will put in my box,

A lightning bolt from the roughest storm
A tongue of fire from a dragon's cave.

I will put in my box,

An evil cackle from a wicked witch
A bite from a cobra, deadly.

I will put in my box,

A silver cloud from another world
A pot of gold from the end of the rainbow.

I will put in my box,

A flutter from a fairy's wings
A voice from an angel, soft and sweet.

My box is made of ice and snow from
the tip of Mount Everest and some glowing gems
from a dragon's lair with some sharks' teeth for decoration.

I will keep it in the centre of the Earth.

Jordan Cook (9)
St Mary's Catholic Primary School, Newtown

MY HIDDEN TREASURES

I keep someone very special
And talk to her every day
Her name is called Smily
She keeps everything I say.

I share all the secrets I have
Smily would keep them as her treasure
She would never be sad
Because I would make her smile in pleasure.

Smily thinks about me
She would never say a sin
I always keep her in safety
I would never chuck her in the bin.

Christina Cachia (10)
St Mary's Catholic Primary School, Newton

MY MUM

My mum is
    a give-you-fruit-when-hungry,
    kind of mum.

She is
    a read-you-a-story-when-you're-scared,
    a play-a-game-with-me,
    kind of mum.

She is
    a get-you-a-flower,
    a go-out-on-her-bicycle,
    a spend-time-with-me,
    kind of mum.

She is
    a tuck-you-in-bed,
    a bug-hunter,
    a funky,
    a jolly,
    kind of mum.

She's an everything kind of mum
and she's all mine.

Lewis Selby (8)
St Mary's Catholic Primary School, Newtown

MY SISTER

My sister is
a kiss-goodbye-before-going-into-her-classroom,
    kind of sister.

My sister is
a sister-to-play-with
a sister-to-have-fun-with,
    kind of sister.

My sister is
a sister-that-comes-in-my-bed-in-the-morning
a sister-to-watch-Stuart-Little-and-the-Rugrats-Movie-with
a sister-to-play-outside-with,
    kind of sister.

My sister is
a sister-to-have-sleepovers-with
a sister-to-read-stories-to
a sister-to-be-friendly-with
a sister-to-be-happy-with,
    kind of sister,

        and she's my sister always.

Megan O'Brien (8)
St Mary's Catholic Primary School, Newtown

MY GRANDAD

My gramp is
a Gramp-will-fix-it
kind of grandad

He is
a pick-me-up-after-school,
a pop-to-Do-it-All-to-get-me-a-woodcraft-tool
kind of grandad

He is
a go-to-the-park-to-have-some-fun
a do-you-want-a-nice-cream-bun?
a would-you-like-some-chocolate-cake
kind of grandad

He is
a look-after-you-when-Mum's-away
a don't-worry-about-the-sweets-I'll-pay
a give-me-a-cake-when-I'm-hungry
a cool-me-down-when-I'm-angry
kind of grandad.

Gregory Barrett (9)
St Mary's Catholic Primary School, Newtown

A COLOUR POEM

What is yellow?
    Happiness is yellow, joyful, cheerful and caring.

What is green?
    Envy is green, jealousy, spite and bitterness.

What is blue?
    Sadness is blue, upset, down-hearted and gloomy.

What is grey?
    A castle, welcoming, tall and proud.

What is silver?
    A rocket is silver, blasting into space.

What is white?
    A dove is white flying up in the clear sky.

What is black?
    Big storm clouds coming over.

Naomi Jane Williams (7)
St Mary's Catholic Primary School, Newtown

MY MUM

My mum is
A give-you-an-apple-when-you're-hungry
Kind of mum.

She is
A give-you-a-hug-and-kiss
A pick-me-up-from-school
Kind of mum.

She is
A happy-jolly-mum
A let's-go-to-the-beach
A let's-bake-a-cake
Kind of mum.

She is
A how-would-you-like-a-chocolate?
A read-you-a-bedtime-story
A give-you-ice cream
A loving-and-caring
Kind of mum.

She's loving and she's all mine.

Sammie Lloyd (9)
St Mary's Catholic Primary School, Newtown

A RUSTY BIT OF METAL

My friend and I have a treasure
That's buried underground
We buried it years ago
And we can't find it now.

If we find it now we'll be sad
Because Dad will be bad
And Mum will be mad
Because it's just a bit of rusty metal.

It gave us good luck
And now our luck is bad
We wish we hadn't dug it up
Because we have gone mad.

Joshua Pearson (10)
St Mary's Catholic Primary School, Newtown

MY OLD ONE PENCE

I treasure an old one pence,
I found it in a fence,
I keep it in my room
where my mum does not loom.

I treasure an old one pence,
I found it in a fence,
I forgot it was there,
until I found it under a chair.

I treasure an old one pence,
I found it in a fence,
I took it to my nan's one day
and left it there until May.

I treasure an old one pence,
I found it in a fence,
I got my one pence back,
and then I broke my back.

A very old man came the next day,
he asked me for a penny,
I gave him my special penny,
the one I treasured so much,
I didn't see the man again
but my back had no more pain.

Reece Moles (9)
St Mary's Catholic Primary School, Newtown

YOU'RE A ...

You're a black night sky
shining above me.

You're a yellow sun in the
morning light, shining bright

You're a beat of a big base drum

You're a brown twinkling tambourine

You're a fishy fish finger

You're a soft and lovely person,
you're my mum.

You're a spicy and juicy glass of juice

You're a long-sleeved jacket too big
for me, made out of leather

You're a city as big as London

You're a feeling that is warm.

Todd Reading (8)
St Mary's Catholic Primary School, Newton

SPECIAL TREASURE

I treasure an old five pence
Found up in the loft.
I keep it in a special box
Wrapped in cotton soft.

I treasure an old five pence
Found up in the attic.
It's lost, I thought
And now I'm out with naught.

I went up in the attic
And I got my five pence
Which was very dusty
I really, really love my five pence.

I treasure an old five pence
I play with it and play with it,
Even in a sandpit,
And now I will make sure I keep it.

Aidan Parry (9)
St Mary's Catholic Primary School, Newtown

MY MAGIC BOX

I will put into my box,

a joke of my uncle's that will make me laugh
and a cuddle from my mum.

I will put into my box,

a supper for me so I won't go hungry
and a silver cloud full of happiness.

I will put into my box,

a tear of joy playing with my friends.

I will put into my box,
some muddy and dusty dinosaur bones
and a rattling snake.

My box will be made out of gold and silver
twinkling brightly like a diamond.

I will keep my box on Big Ben.

Ashley Parry (8)
St Mary's Catholic Primary School, Newtown

A COLOUR POEM?

What is pink?
Love is pink, spreading across the world.

What is yellow?
Happiness is yellow, shining for more.

What is white?
A start of a dream drifting through your mind is white.

What is red?
Anger is red, cross and hot.

What is green?
Leaves are green, bristling through the wind.

What is black?
A twilight darkness, spinning through your head is black.

Amber Shanahan (8)
St Mary's Catholic Primary School, Newtown

THE STORM

Leaves swaying, wind gently blowing,
Branches rustling, birds screeching,
Animals running, clouds forming.

Thunder, *roaring, banging,*
Lightning, *flashing, bashing,*
Sea, *mashing, crashing,*
Wind, *savaging,* people *screaming*
Rain, *spraying, flooding.*

Clouds are disappearing.
People aren't screaming
Branches calmly sway.

Ceri Brown (8)
St Mary's Catholic Primary School, Newtown

MY AMAZING SHELL

I treasure an amazing shell
That I can describe very well
That I found with my mum
On the seashore bed.

My amazing shell that I treasure
Gives me lots of pleasure
I keep it in my room
Where my mum will not clean
                    with her broom
It gives me good luck
That I will never lose
This will always be my hidden treasure
That will give me lots of pleasure.

Alex Bacigalupo (9)
St Mary's Catholic Primary School, Newtown

THE STORM

Leaves rustling, wind whistling,
raindrops falling, branches swaying,
letter boxes rattling, animals fleeing,
birds screeching.

Lighting slashing, trashing, thunder lashing,
trees crashing, houses falling, darkness drawing
sea crashing, rain stinging, rivers flooding,
wind savaging, people fleeing,
hailstones now falling, falling.

Rainbows appearing, clouds disappearing,
animals returning, people celebrating.
Soon the sun will be rising.

William Reynolds (8)
St Mary's Catholic Primary School, Newtown

THE KEY THAT DOESN'T FIT

Up in the attic I found a key,
hmmm, wonder where it fits,
wherever that may be?

Not in the front door,
Not in the back,
Where is the secret door that I lack?

Maybe it's the key for a trapdoor
or a secret passage hidden in the floor?

If this is true, there must be treasure,
gold, silver, a skeleton that's hundreds
of years old.

The key doesn't fit anywhere,
so I'll treasure the key,
until I find a door that fits.

Luke Bacigalupo (11)
St Mary's Catholic Primary School, Newtown

HAPPINESS IS . . .

Happiness is playing football,
Happiness is ice cream,
Happiness is snow that falls,
Happiness is Christmas dinner,
Happiness is full of joy,
Happiness is a warm bed,
Happiness is special people,
Happiness is being proud of your work,
Happiness is a pet dog,
Happiness is a friend to play with,
Happiness is birthdays.

Vanessa Parkin (8)
St Mary's Catholic Primary School, Newtown

MY HIDDEN TREASURE

I have this old, old teddy,
I love this old, old teddy.
When I wake up, I wake up with her.

When I come from school,
I know she is waiting for me.
I love my old, old teddy.

She is a white teddy with silky ears
and a nice dress with roses on it.

When I go to sleep, she keeps me safe
And I keep her safe.
I take her with me everywhere I go.

I call her Daisy.
I love my old teddy,
I really, really do.

Marisa Buckly-Robins (9)
St Mary's Catholic Primary School, Newtown

MY TEDDY TREASURE

My teddy is my treasure,
I love him very much,
I tell him all my secrets,
When I'm mad or sad.

I take him everywhere I go,
Except to school, of course.

I treasure him and love him
And will keep him forever and ever.

Hannah Cook (11)
St Mary's Catholic Primary School, Newtown

TREASURE IN A SHIP

I went down into the sea,
Minding my own business,
And swimming happily.

Then it all went dark,
There, showing its teeth,
In the gloom, was a shark.

There was a dolphin, so very small,
It took me to shore,
So I gave it my ball.

My family and I started to walk
And what did we find?
An old ship,
We went inside.

There was treasure,
In a chest,
We'll remember this day forever.

Emma Cook (10)
St Mary's Catholic Primary School, Newtown

THE SECRET DOOR

All my life I've wondered on,
What could be upon,
The hidden passageway.
What could be behind the 'secret door'
Gold and silver or money galore
A magic door, to a mystic land,
Powerful crystals,
Diamonds and jewels? Oh well,
I'll just have to wait and see.

Edward Raprager (10)
St Mary's Catholic Primary School, Newtown

YOU'RE A ...

You're a song of a robin,
in an oak tree.

You're a red, red rose,
sparkling in the sun.

You're a chocolate cake,
with white delicious cream on top.

You're a flame,
burning brightly.

You're a can of fizzy orange,
running down my throat.

        You're my mum.

Taran Buckley-Robins (7)
St Mary's Catholic Primary School, Newtown

MY TEDDY BEAR

My teddy bear is my treasure
I play with him with pleasure
He's my best teddy bear
I sometimes take him to the fair
Yes, he's my best teddy bear.

My teddy bear sleeps at the bottom of my bed
Once he hurt his head on the bed
Then I said, 'Don't worry I will help you.'
Yes, he's my best teddy bear.

I like my teddy bear because he's my treasure
He's called Snowy.

Sarah McNally Benson (9)
St Mary's Catholic Primary School, Newtown

THE SEASONS

Summer
Eat ice cream on the sandy beach
scorching hot holidays!
Blue water to swim in the sun
people thirsty, dry mouths.

Autumn
Autumn leaves drop from their trees
green leaves on the ground
blowing frantically on the playground
fruit on the huge tree.

Spring
Flowers open in the sunshine
newborn lambs run very fast
waking up, the sunlight shining on me
weeds open from the ground

Winter
Blowing fog while the cold rains fall
snowball fights in the streets
eating chocolate out of doors
Christmas is good for all.

Katie Ensall (11)
Sandycroft CP School, Deeside

BARBADOS

The purple sea, as still as a flower in the Caribbean sun,
having a great time on the surfboard, great fun.
People on the beach as still as the sun, lying in peace,
children playing beach soccer on the golden sand,
jet skis floating on the calm sea, great fun!

James Hurlin (10)
Sandycroft CP School, Deeside

FEELINGS

Touch the smoothness of a pony's coat
And the roughness of a pony's mane
Can you feel the pony's hooves hammering the ground?
And stroke a horse
The feeling of a dolphin reminds me of the waves
To handle the reins of a pony galloping
Makes me feel happy
But best feeling of all is the pony
I like to touch his mane as the wind blows in my face.

Layla Davies (7)
Sandycroft CP School, Deeside

POEM FOR SPRINGTIME

In the springtime I can see
Birds tweeting in the sky.

Next I can see sheep leaping in the grass,
And I can see flowers growing in the field,
And I can see a squirrel climbing up a tree.

I can hear a fox sneaking in the leaves.

Dylan Thomas & Liam Scott (7)
Sandycroft CP School, Deeside

A POEM FOR SPRINGTIME

In the springtime I can see daffodils in the growing grass.
In the springtime I can see lambs dancing for me.
In the springtime I can see grasshoppers jumping on me.
In the springtime I can hear the birds singing on the pier.

Corey Peers (8)
Sandycroft CP School, Deeside

SEASONS

Autumn
Trees are green and help us to breathe
Trees for fruit, trees for shade
Autumn trees lose their crunchy leaves
And see their beauty fade.

Winter
As the winter carpet takes over
Children have snowball fights
Slip on the ice, slip on the snow.

Spring
See flowers, see newborn lambs and calves
See the lambs running about
See the lambs waking and the sheep
Plant the bulbs, watch them grow.

Summer
Rush to the beach, make sandcastles
See your ice cream melting
Put the sunblock on, *brrr*, it's cold
Watch the sunblock soak in.

Luke Ames (10)
Sandycroft CP School, Deeside

THE POND

So round and beautiful
And in the park,
Somewhere near me,
There's a singing lark.

The happy shouts of children
Coming from around me,
Looking in the pond
Lots of water creatures are what I see.

Fish, water snails, there are also worms,
Everything you can think of.
But wait, there's a little bee,
Get out and buzz off!

Oh look, it's got out now . . .
Wait, is it going to sting me?
I hope not, oh wait, I've got to go,
I really do, 'Goodbye, bee.'

Leanne Jones (10)
Sandycroft CP School, Deeside

SEASONS OF THE YEAR

Trees are green and help us to breathe
Trees for fruit, trees for shade
Autumn trees lose their crunchy leaves
And see their beauty fade.

Our surrounding, our environment
Keep it clean, protect it
Treat it with care, love it.

Illuminated houses bright
Christmas trees are glowing
Christmas brings wonderful presents
Christmas is so icy.

Flowers, bulbs, gently growing
Bright sunshine, daffodils
Newborn animals greet the world.

Punch and Judy on the pier
Barbecue on the sand
Eating candyfloss by blue sea
Children worship the sun.

Hannah Day (10)
Sandycroft CP School, Deeside

THE FOREST

The trees sway as the chilly wind brushes the leaves
And the flowers shake in the rhythm,
The birds sing, like it's spring,
But it's the cold, chilly autumn.

The forest is dark, like the dead of night,
Grasshoppers chirping like baby birds,
Glow-worms form a circle,
Like a glow in the dark, watch!

As the morning dawns,
Light creeps through gaps in the trees,
Like light finding its way through someone's curtains.
Birds start singing and a cockerel says
'Good morning' in the distance.
The squirrels wake and start gathering nuts
                              for breakfast.

Penny Glover (10)
Sandycroft CP School, Deeside

RUNS, RUNS, RUNS

As the ball bounces off the field, wow!
Six
As you hear the noises swish, cheering smack!
Six
As the wickets fall one by one, it's still a
Six!
As the fielders gaze at the ball
Six
As the bowlers' amazed faces turn
Six! Six! Six!

Sam Fairgrieve (11)
Sandycroft CP School, Deeside

IN THE SPRING

In the springtime I can see
Sparkling water on the sea,

Baby lambs bleating
Under a tree,

Dolphins clicking
In the sea,

Buds growing
In the tree.

In the springtime I can hear
The sound of the breeze
And birdsong
Coming to my ear.

Vanessa Ward & Rebekah Gleadhill (8)
Sandycroft CP School, Deeside

SOUNDS

I love the sound of cats purring
When I'm at home
I like to hear the ocean splash
And the barking of dogs
As I go to sleep.
The sound of sizzling sausages
When I wake up in the morning
Makes me feel starving,
But the sound that I like the best of all
Is the leaves falling off the trees

Because it is nice and peaceful.

Michael Hughes (8)
Sandycroft CP School, Deeside

MY BEDROOM

This is where I play on my computer,
Read books and sleep at night.
I think it is warm and cosy.
It's a special place for me.

I had a dream last night,
It was a funny place to be.
I was at the circus
Making people laugh.

It makes me feel happy,
Just sitting there alone,
Playing on my computer
On Art Attack.

Cassandra Weston-Laing (10)
Sandycroft CP School, Deeside

POEM FOR SPRINGTIME

In the springtime I can see
Lambs eating and bleating
In the spring breeze.

In the springtime I can hear
People shouting, 'Hooray!'
On the big road.

In the springtime I can smell
Long trees growing leaves
And blossom buds.

Anthony Carrino (8)
Sandycroft CP School, Deeside (7)

SPRING

In the springtime I can see
Dogs sniffing the green grass
Fish swimming in the pond
Caterpillars climbing up the trees
To nibble the leaves
Cats coming out to play in fresh air

In the springtime I can hear
The breeze blowing through the trees
Birds singing in the sky
Chicks learning how to fly
Lambs bleating in the fresh air

In the springtime I can smell
The air as it blows in different directions
Flowers as they are growing
Plants as ants march around them
Buds when they begin to grow

In the springtime I can feel
The air as it blows gently on my face
The soft wool of the sheep as they lie in the field
The leaves of the blowing trees
And the pretty flowers of the Earth.

Daniel Massey
Sandycroft CP School, Deeside

ALCUDIA

As the sun slowly goes down,
the whole world just drifts away.
The sand on the bare beaches
drags itself along gently.
The town square goes from noisy to silent,
as the dead of night comes.
As morning breaks,
the noise comes with it,
noisy little feet,
and little chatty mouths.
The beachgoers rise,
Towels are laid,
get your bucket and spade,
and a net,
you might just catch a fish.
As it gets hot
you start to sweat.
Restaurants and bars are full.
Seagulls are gliding in the air.
Candyfloss, chocolate and
ice cream at the fair.
As time passes, the beaches go silent
and it starts all over again.

Louise Rowlands-Bell (10)
Sandycroft CP School, Deeside

MY HOLIDAY

Aqua pool with rushing water,
Rubber ring floating like birds
bobbing on the sea.
The rushing water joins to the
big pool, erupting as they meet.

Noise around as mums and dads
relax in the sun.
Music blaring, children shouting
and loudspeaker announcements.
Memories from my holiday.
I wish I was still there.

Charlette Egan (10)
Sandycroft CP School, Deeside

SEASONS POEM

Winter
Cold snow in my hair, frosty snow
Frosty streets, snowball fights
Children have snow fights on cold ice
Christmas Day, frosty ice.

Spring
Joy in spring, little cute lambs are born
See the baby lambs asleep
See all the lambs eating the flowers
More daylight, more lambs wake.

Summer
Bright hot sunshine blazing all day
On the beach, hear the birds
Cheerful nice people in the blue water
Seeing the bright blue water.

Autumn
Trees are green and help us breathe
Trees for fruit, trees for shade
Autumn trees lose their crunchy leaves
And see their beauty fade.

Stefanie Louise Morgan (10)
Sandycroft CP School, Deeside

MY FAVOURITE PLACE

My favourite place is just for me.
My favourite place is dark and light.
My favourite place is warm.
My favourite place is where I do secret things.

My favourite
            place
                is
                    my room!

Sammy Jo Price (12)
Sandycroft CP School, Deeside

SIX WAYS OF LOOKING AT A GARDEN SHED

It looks like a workman's hut on the side of the road.
It is a seaside chalet on the end of the beach.
It is the largest dog's house in our street - *wow!*
It resembles a little shop, with a man in the park selling sweets etc.
It looks like a greenhouse with no glass.
It is a house for a family of dwarfs.

Warren Jones (11)
Sandycroft CP School, Deeside

LOOKING AT A TREE

Trees look like a small mountain with pointed grass.
Trees look like a funny-shaped pencil.
Trees look like stick people with frizzy hair.
Trees look like my mum's hair when she wakes up in the morning.
The branches of a tree look like giants' babies' fingers.
When trees are together, they look like people fighting.

Jonathon Johnston (11)
Sandycroft CP School, Deeside

WEST KIRBY BEACH

Step onto the golden sand,
With squiggly blustering sand under my feet,
With rocks and grains of shells,
Water splashing, birds' wings flapping noisily,
Children riding . . . on donkeys' backs,
Seagulls screeching
The tide flows . . .
No rocks, no shells, no donkeys . . .
Step into the sparkling sea.

Tania Williams (10)
Sandycroft CP School, Deeside

SIX WAYS OF LOOKING AT THE SUN . . .

It looks like a fire on a beach barbecue,
It looks like a huge football,
It's a bowl of red tomatoes,
It's like golden earrings in a jewellery shop,
It is like a marble from the bottom of my garden,
It looks like a clock ticking contentedly.

Lauren Jones (11)
Sandycroft CP School, Deeside

THERE WAS AN OLD GHOST FROM THE WEST

There was an old ghost from the west
Who was a bit of a pest
She cast a nasty spell
And off the cliff she fell
That silly old ghost from the west.

Daniel Hallett (11)
Tonysguboriau Primary School, Pontyclun

CREAKING ON THE STAIRS

Screams in the basement
Mysterious shadows in the hallway
Eyes like crystal in the garden
Footsteps in the garden
Screaming in the garden, help!
Help . . . !

Stephen Woodland (10)
Tonysguboriau Primary School, Pontyclun

BLOOD-BOILING BEWITCHMENTS

Blood-boiling bewitchments
Gloomy grumpy ghosts
Wicked wolves weeping
Sick spooky spectres
Horribly haunting hooligans
Mouths murmuring murder.

Sam Evans (11)
Tonysguboriau Primary School, Pontyclun

EYES GLOWING LIKE FIRE

Eyes glowing like fire.
Demons watching in the dark.
Ghostly footsteps in the corridor.
Cobwebs in the corner.
Constantly creaking floorboards
Knife-cutting wind blowing through the cracks.
Shadows creeping across the wall.

William Rees-Crockford (10)
Tonysguboriau Primary School, Pontyclun

SCREAMS FROM THE BASEMENT

Screams from the basement
Bloodthirsty wolves howling
Mysterious voices haunting
Ghostly shadows creeping
Coffins creaking in the distance
Chills in the night air
Creaks from the doors
Horribly haunting houses.

Libby Anderson (10)
Tonysguboriau Primary School, Pontyclun

GLOOMY NOISY NIGHTS

Gloomy noisy nights
Invisible ghosts creeping
Silent spooky shadows
Creepy haunted houses
Horrible tattered coffins
Skeletons like ghostly spirits.

Samantha Dean (10)
Tonysguboriau Primary School, Pontyclun

THERE WAS A DOG OF THE NIGHT

There was a dog of the night
Who had a very good fright
He looked out of the door
And saw a skeleton on the floor
That was the dog of the night.

Nathan Ellis (10)
Tonysguboriau Primary School, Pontyclun

SPOOKY HAUNTED HOUSES

Spooky haunted houses
Gloomy ghostly nights
Misty eyes are coming, shall I run away?
Creepy frightening noises
Screaming in the room
Misty spirits lurking, hiding in the dark
Silent ghosts are moving, creeping down the stairs.

Zöe Beynon (10)
Tonysguboriau Primary School, Pontyclun

THERE WAS A GHOST FROM SOUTH WALES

There was a ghost from South Wales
Who had some very, very long nails

He flew through the air
Taking very good care

That scary old ghost from South Wales.

Abbie Ingham (11)
Tonysguboriau Primary School, Pontyclun

THE OLD GHOUL

There was an old ghoul of the south
Who couldn't open his mouth
He glued it together
In some foggy weather
That silly old ghoul of the south.

Chris Thomas (10)
Tonysguboriau Primary School, Pontyclun

THE DARK NIGHT WAS A FRIGHT

There were screams in the basement
Footsteps on the garden path
There were bony screeches on the door
Wolves howling, bats shrieking
There was a long silence
Then a scream
Holes through the walls
Pots smashing
Skeletons coming out of the earth
Coffins in the hallway
Then a bang!
Blood everywhere
Laughing, day and night
Such a frightening sight.

Andre Merrick (10)
Tonysguboriau Primary School, Pontyclun

THE FISH AND THE CAT

I have a fish who lives in a dish,
He likes to shout and wiggle about,
When he turns on the light he has a big fright,
He learnt to fly in the sky but then fell into the well,

I have a cat who is very fat,
He sleeps in a hat on the mat,
If he is bored he chases a toad,
His best toy is a Game Boy,
But when he dies, he's still got more lives.

Samuel Pritchard (9) & Joshua Beach (10)
Ysgol Gynradd Gymraeg Tonyrefail, Porth

MY BABY SISTER!

I have a baby sister
And I always like to kiss her
She's small and chubby
And her bum is very flubby
It wobbles when she walks
And she babbles when she talks
I like my baby sister because
she's very funny
Especially when she wees over
my mummy!

When it's time for bed she screams until
she turns red
She thinks it very funny when she
clonks me on the head
The only time she makes me unhappy
Is when she fills her nappy
But I'll love my sister always
Right up until I'm dead.

Tim Harvey (10)
Ysgol Gynradd Gymraeg Tonyrefail, Porth

MY PETS

I have a kitten called George.
He likes to think he's tough
but he's really a big ball of fluff.
His favourite food is chicken
and his milk dish he likes lickin'.

Fred, Barney and Dino.
One, two, three
these fish belong to me.
I bought them for a pound
and they like to swim around.

My hamster's name is Jack.
He's coloured white and black.
Jack runs around in his cage
when he's in a rage
and then he falls asleep.

Polly and Du-Du are twelve years old
and never do what they're told.
One's skinny, one's fat,
they sleep on the mat
and both are very nice cats.

Celyn Ferris (10)
Ysgol Gynradd Gymraeg Tonyrefail, Porth

THE DAYS OF THE WEEK

Monday was very busy,
Tuesday was very silly,
Wednesday was incredibly funny,
Thursday was, oh no!
Friday was hip, hip, hooray,
Saturday was boring!
Sunday was a very lazy day.

There can be lots of things
Throughout the week
Some funny, some silly,
But at the end of the week,
Everybody goes hip, hip, hooray!

My dogs are not lazy,
No not really,
But, oh yes, I have a kitten who's very lazy
And very silly.

Teya Kiff (10)
Ysgol Gynradd Gymraeg Tonyrefail, Porth

TIGER, TIGER!

Your stripes flash,
Out your claws lash.

I catch a glimpse of
your golden fur,
You can run very fast and
contentedly purr.

You run after prey
mile by mile.
You scavenge one
in a while.

I adore you, tiger,
but you will always be
a fierce
predator!

Catherine Evans (11)
Ysgol Gynradd Gymraeg Tonyrefail, Porth

MY LIFE

My life is all about rugby
I think about it all the time
Except when I'm scoring a try
I watch it nearly every day
Well, that's what my father says
I read about it page to page
I've liked it since I was six years of age
I like to hear some rugby tales
Especially when it's
about Wales.

Alex Whitehead (11)
Ysgol Gynradd Gymraeg Tonyrefail, Porth

MY DOG MAX

My dog Max,
He chases cats
And barks when he wants to play.

He plays with his toy,
He's a really good boy
And sits when I tell him to stay.

He chases his tail
And eats the mail
And goes for long walks with my dad.

He's black and tan
And a big Alsation.
He's the best friend I've ever had.

Ffion Edwards (11)
Ysgol Gynradd Gymraeg Tonyrefail, Porth

MY TEN DOGS

My ten dogs.
They are soft and cuddly.
But sometimes they get mucky,
And my mother does not like it at all.
But still we always love them.

My ten dogs.
They can be noisy.
They can be quiet.
They can be naughty.
They can be good.
But still we always love them.

Bethan Williams (10)
Ysgol Gynradd Gymraeg Tonyrefail, Porth

My China Doll

My china doll is very pretty,
And her hands are so dainty.
She likes to stare everywhere.

She sits on the shelf
All day and all night.
Sometimes she gives me a big fright
When her face glows up with
The bright, white moon
That makes a shadow all over the room.
She has a fixed stare
And watches you when you're unaware.

Elin Jones (10)
Ysgol Gynradd Gymraeg Tonyrefail, Porth

My Funny Ferret

My funny ferret, he lives in the shed,
He climbs up my trousers all the way to my head.

He plays with his bell, he plays with his ball,
He plays with me, I'm best of all.

He wakes up in the morning, but stays in bed,
Until someone comes to stroke his head.

I love him and he loves me,
We both agree on eggs for tea.

Kelly-Louise Williams (10)
Ysgol Gynradd Gymraeg Tonyrefail, Porth

MY NEPHEW

My little nephew who is two years old,
he never does what he's been told.
He never sleeps at all at night,
he always wants to play and fight.

He plays until it's time for bed,
and never rests his sleepy head.
His hair's so curly, oh, so curly,
he always gets out of bed early.

He runs around all the time,
he never stops, it's such a crime.
He always breaks a toy,
because he's such a naughty boy.

Amy Llewellyn (10)
Ysgol Gynradd Gymraeg Tonyrefail, Porth

IN MY FUTURE

In my future cars might fly,
Computers with legs could pass us by,
If I could live up in space
It could be just ace.

Interactive teachers on TV
How brilliant that would be,
Learning at home, not going to school,
Chilling at home, not losing your cool.

Aaron Daye (11)
Ysgol Gynradd Gymraeg Tonyrefail, Porth

MARTYN

M y friend when I'm lonely.

A lways willing to listen.

R eady to help me if I am stuck.

T here is nothing he won't share.

Y ou can have fun with him.

N ever lets me down.

Shaun Harrison (10)
Ysgol Gynradd Gymraeg Tonyrefail, Porth

THE PERFECT CHRISTMAS GIFT

Christmas is a happy time,
Of joy, peace and love,
When Jesus Christ, the Saviour,
Descended from God above.

Oh, what happiness, oh, what joy,
There was on seeing that special boy,
The angels shouted, the Wise Men sang hymns,
Upon seeing the Lord,
The King of Kings.

He was born, He lived,
He died for you and me,
Our sins they died with Him,
On a hill at Calvary.

So what is the message,
In my poem you might say?
Well, Jesus is for always
And not just one day.

Carys Thomas, Bethan Woods
& Owain Llyr Williams (11)
Ysgol Gynradd Gymraeg, Castellau

ENDLESS NIGHTMARE

Panting, panting, as I ran through the night,
From a pack of bloodthirsty wolves,
Who had me in their sight.

As I ran from the terror,
The end of the nightmare seemed in sight,
Was the horror over,
Or was I about to have another fright?

My eyes filled with fear,
As I trembled with pain,
I looked up and gasped,
'Oh no, those wolves have found me again.'

I began to run,
My heart filled with fright,
Those beasts were getting closer,
They had me in their sight.

Just as I panicked,
And thought, they've got me,
I'm done
My alarm started to shake,
My nightmare's over,
'Oh yes, I'm awake,
I've won, I've won.'

Carys Thomas (11)
Ysgol Gynradd Gymraeg, Castellau

LOST IN SPACE!

Zooming through galaxies
Black holes galore
Most of us wishing
And hoping for more.

Scientists say
There's a new planet about
'He's called Planet X!'
The words come in a shout.

Zooming past Mars
Flying through Pluto
No sign of cars
Or major paluto.

Floating around
Like a big fat balloon
But I'm really supposed
To be exploring the moon.

'Houston! We have a problem!'
Thundered the radio
The black holes will gobble 'em!
Are the odds of the ratio.

That's enough fun
For this Apollo mission
Now we can go home,
For the space competition.

Bethan Woods (11)
Ysgol Gynradd Gymraeg, Castellau